AF827319

Bargaining over Time Allocation

Contributions to Economics

http://www.springer.de/cgi-bin/search_book.pl?series=1262

Sardar M. N. Islam
Mathematical Economics of Multi-Level Optimisation
1998. ISBN 3-7908-1050-9

Sven-Morten Mentzel
Real Exchange Rate Movements
1998. ISBN 3-7908-1081-9

Lei Delsen/Eelke de Jong (Eds.)
The German and Dutch Economies
1998. ISBN 3-7908-1064-9

Mark Weder
Business Cycle Models with Indeterminacy
1998. ISBN 3-7908-1078-9

Tor Rødseth (Ed.)
Models for Multispecies Management
1998. ISBN 3-7908-1001-0

Michael Carlberg
Intertemporal Macroeconomics
1998. ISBN 3-7908-1096-7

Sabine Spangenberg
The Institutionalised Transformation of the East German Economy
1998. ISBN 3-7908-1103-3

Hagen Bobzin
Indivisibilities
1998. ISBN 3-7908-1123-8

Helmut Wagner (Ed.)
Current Issues in Monetary Economics
1998. ISBN 3-7908-1127-0

Peter Michaelis/Frank Stähler (Eds.)
Recent Policy Issues in Environmental and Resource Economics
1998. ISBN 3-7908-1137-8

Jessica de Wolff
The Political Economy of Fiscal Decisions
1998. ISBN 3-7908-1130-0

Georg Bol/Gholamreza Nakhaeizadeh/Karl-Heinz Vollmer (Eds.)
Risk Measurements, Econometrics and Neural Networks
1998. ISBN 3-7908-1152-1

Joachim Winter
Investment and Exit Decisions at the Plant Level
1998. ISBN 3-7908-1154-8

Bernd Meyer
Intertemporal Asset Pricing
1999. ISBN 3-7908-1159-9

Uwe Walz
Dynamics of Regional Integration
1999. ISBN 3-7908-1185-8

Michael Carlberg
European Monetary Union
1999. ISBN 3-7908-1191-2

Giovanni Galizzi/Luciano Venturini (Eds.)
Vertical Relationships and Coordination in the Food System
1999. ISBN 3-7908-1192-0

Gustav A. Horn/Wolfgang Scheremet/Rudolf Zwiener
Wages and the Euro
1999. ISBN 3-7908-1199-8

Dirk Willer
The Development of Equity Capital Markets in Transition Economies
1999. ISBN 3-7908-1198-X

Karl Matthias Weber
Innovation Diffusion and Political Control of Energy Technologies
1999. ISBN 3-7908-1205-6

Heike Link et al.
The Costs of Road Infrastructure and Congestion in Europe
1999. ISBN 3-7908-1201-3

Simon Duindam
Military Conscription
1999. ISBN 3-7908-1203-X

Bruno Jeitziner
Political Economy of the Swiss National Bank
1999. ISBN 3-7908-1209-9

Irene Ring et al. (Eds.)
Regional Sustainability
1999. ISBN 3-7908-1233-1

continued on page 140

Miriam Beblo

Bargaining over Time Allocation

Economic Modeling and Econometric Investigation of Time Use within Families

Physica-Verlag
A Springer-Verlag Company

Series Editors
Werner A. Müller
Martina Bihn

Author
Dr. Miriam Beblo
Zentrum für
Europäische Wirtschaftsforschung (ZEW)
Forschungsbereich Arbeitsmärkte, Personalmanagement
und Soziale Sicherung
L 7,1
68161 Mannheim
Deutschland
E-mail: beblo@zew.de

ISSN 1431-1933
ISBN 3-7908-1391-5 Physica-Verlag Heidelberg New York

D188 (2000)

Cataloging-in-Publication Data applied for
Die Deutsche Bibliothek – CIP-Einheitsaufnahme
Beblo, Miriam: Bargaining over time allocation: economic modeling and econometric investigation of time use within families / Miriam Beblo. – Heidelberg; New York: Physica-Verl., 2001
(Contributions to economics)
Zugl.: Berlin, Freie Univ., Diss., 1999
ISBN 3-7908-1391-5

Physica-Verlag Heidelberg New York
a member of BertelsmannSpringer Science+Business Media GmbH

Softcover Design: Erich Kirchner, Heidelberg

SPIN 10797439 88/2202-5 4 3 2 1 0 – Printed on acid-free and non-aging paper

Acknowledgements

I have written this dissertational thesis while being a research and teaching assistant at the Institute of Public Finance and Social Policy at Freie Universität in Berlin. The thesis has been completed in December 1999. Having studied bargaining behavior in greater detail now, I must say that my work has benefitted from cooperation of those who accompanied my research during the past five years. First of all I would like to thank my advisors Irwin L. Collier and Notburga Ott for their constant encouragement and precious comments. In presentations and stimulating discussions I also received valuable input from my colleagues at Freie Universität Berlin as well as professors and fellow students at the graduate college "Applied Microeconomics". Most importantly, I am grateful to my husband Sven Ammerlahn for his inspiring and incredibly patient support.

Contents

1 Introduction

KARL MARX 1857:

Ökonomie der Zeit, darein löst sich schließlich alle Ökonomie auf.

(Economy of time, to this all economy ultimately reduces itself.)

GARY S. BECKER 1993:

Different constraints are decisive for different situations, but the most fundamental constraint is limited time.

1.1 Time allocation in a bargaining family

In modern economic theories of time allocation three major groups of time uses are generally distinguished: paid (market) labor, unpaid (household) labor and leisure. In modern economic theories of family decision making household behavior is typically modeled as the outcome of a bargaining process between family members who bargain over household resource allocation and the intrafamily distribution of welfare. In the chapters to follow both "approaches" will be emphasized to study time use behavior within households. Such bargaining models of family decision making will be seen to pose a challenge to traditional time allocation theory.

Four theoretical and empirical studies constitute the contribution of this dissertation to explain trends such as rising female employment, particularly that of women with small children, along with falling fertility rates and increasing divorce rates. My purpose is to shed light on the division of housework between spouses and the observed leisure differential between women and men. Bargaining models provide new insights into the internal organization and structure of the black box family. This is not merely a matter of methodology but facilitates goal-oriented policy recommendations. Where standard models of the household would offer misleading conclusions about the effects of public policy on the behavior of household members regarded individually due to an (over-)simplifying assumption that households act as welfare maximizing units, bargaining models allow us to focus on the relative advantages and disadvantages of members of a household.

We begin with the definition of distinct time uses as analyzed throughout the thesis. This is followed by a discussion of the notion of family from an economic perspective. In the third part of this introductory chapter the general structure of the dissertation and the research focuses of its four component studies will be stretched.

1.2 Time use

Time allocation theory models three major time uses: market labor, household labor and leisure. The general term labor refers to all activities that are inputs in the production of output which can be transferred between individuals. In other words, labor includes all activities that do not have to be performed by a particular individual. The difference between market labor and household labor relates to the nature of the transactions taking place. Whereas market transactions are typically direct bilateral exchange activities with money as the means of exchange, household transactions are characterized by a high number of goods and services that are typically exchanged between several family members (Ott 1999). Leisure or private time, on the contrary, does not yield any such outputs that could be traded in return for other services. It is defined as time spent on self-determined activities that involve production and consumption taking place at the same time. Since such activities are pursued for their own sake, for the benefit of the individual so to speak, they have to be exclusively performed by that same person. The output is consumed simultaneously and therefore cannot be delegated to anybody else and then transferred, as might be the case with housekeeping or child care. This concept of leisure is called the third person criterion (see Schäfer/Schwarz 1996 and Ott 1999). Sport activities, watching TV or eating and sleeping for instance, since they have to be performed by oneself, are considered leisure activities[1].

Each member of a family regards time as a scarce resource to be allocated among these competing uses. While each member is endowed with the same total amount of time per day or per week, it is the price at which each unit of time is valued that differs across family members. In the economic analysis of time allocation a monetary value reflecting the opportunity cost in terms of market work or household production can be assigned to each unit of time,

[1] This distinction is well illustrated by the following remark from the United Nations' *Human Development Report* (1995: 89): "No one else can eat your breakfast on your behalf or catch up on your sleep."

even if this unit is "spent" on leisure. This monetary value represents the scarcity of the disposable time which will depend on individual efficiency indicators such as hourly wage rates or household productivities. Given these prices, the optimization problem of the family is to determine the most efficient allocation of each member's time, i.e. the division of labor within the household and each individual's quantity of leisure time. We have no need to regard the economic approach to be an exclusive method for analyzing time use. Indeed economic explanations are complementary to those of other social sciences[2].

1.3 The family as an economic institution

The household or the family may be regarded as an institution for human reproduction and where such fundamental needs as love, safety and material security are met. While a family can take on various forms and does not necessarily require a common household, for economic analysis the terms family and household are often used synonymously. Since the focus of this dissertation will be on the production aspect of family time use we will also refer to both terms interchangeably.

Generally the phrase household may apply to any number of people who agree to living together. For simplicity I shall restrict my analysis of intrafamily time allocation to a bargaining process between two individuals assumed to be man and woman; a household setting that still represents the majority of two-adult-headed families. Some of the results can be meaningfully generalized to other household structures as well, be it that of mother and daughter, brother and sister, a homosexual couple or many other possible living arrangements. However, some results, especially those based on gender differences or driven by policy measures, only apply to the traditional family setting assumed here.

The economic institution family constitutes a place of economic production as well as of reproduction. We assume that through such a long-term internal relationship members of a family attain higher welfare levels than could be achieved through market relations alone. By forming a community of production, consumption and insurance the household can avoid transaction costs, that arise with the production and trade of market goods (Ben-Porath 1980, Pollak 1985 and Ott 1993). Transaction costs include information costs, negotiation costs as well as monitoring costs. The social contacts within a family and affections between family members provide informa-

[2] For a general discussion of the economic modeling of time see for instance Biervert/Held (1995b), Biesecker (1995) and other contributions to the book on "Zeit in der Ökonomik" edited by Biervert/Held (1995a).

tional and monitoring advantages that help to lower these costs. By marriage or by informal household formation individuals replace market relationships (e.g. with laundries, restaurants or nannies) with an economic organization that yields gains from long-term cooperation of its members. Through the joint consumption of public goods at the household level they can realize efficiency gains and benefit from economies of scale. As an insurance community the family provides insurance against such risks as illness, unemployment or old age of single household members. As a production cooperation it can exploit the family members' comparative production advantages through specialization in distinct activities or responsibilities. Economies of scope arise, for instance, from taking care of children and doing housework at the same time.

The division of labor and the distribution of resources among family members, however, may not only be the subject of cooperation but also of conflicts within households (Pollak 1985, Sen 1990a). On the one hand, family members cooperate in order to maximize the size of the pie, while on the other hand, they must necessarily compete with each other regarding their individual shares of this pie. Hence, they will negotiate over their respective time uses and the distribution of the gains from cooperation. The use of bargaining models of household behavior allows us to treat family members as distinct individuals with common as well as conflicting interests.

1.4 A reader's guide

The first two chapters of the dissertation provide a brief overview of the existing economic approaches to family decision making as well as of the empirical literature. Starting with the traditional time allocation theory (also called the unitary model) initiated by Becker (1965) and Gronau (1973, 1977) Chapter 2 introduces game theoretic approaches including cooperative, non-cooperative and dynamic bargaining models in a theoretical survey. The third chapter reviews a selection of empirical studies regarding the empirical evidence for hypotheses derived from theoretical models that attempt to explain the division of labor within households and the distribution of resources and returns among family members. The objective of this review is to consider the empirical support for the particular assumptions underlying the unitary approach and those that have been proposed in support of the various models of collective behavior. This review of the literature establishes the context for the chapters to follow. The core of the thesis are four studies of individual time use within a family context. All studies follow the same theoretical concept in which the bargaining framework is applied to different empirical aspects of family time use for employment, household production and leisure. Each study provides a theoretical discussion of the relevant economic approaches, a particular specification or an extension of an existing model and in all but one of the chapters to follow an econometric analysis of the observed time use behavior of German households.

The first of these studies (Chapter 4) is devoted to the strategic aspect of the time use paid labor. It has been motivated by the interplay of the following two trends that have been observed in almost all developed Western countries over the past decades: increasing female labor force participation together with continuously rising divorce rates. Independent of whether the increasing risk of divorce has been caused by higher female labor force participation or whether married women now supply more labor as a consequence of a higher risk of divorce, the decision to work will be argued to involve an aspect of insurance that has been missed by traditional models of household labor supply. It is this insurance aspect that will be incorporated in the analysis of female labor supply in Chapter 4. A dynamic bargaining model of family time use is developed, followed by an investigation of the implications of the theoretical model that have been incorporated into an econometric analysis of female labor supply.

In the dynamic bargaining model time allocation is determined by intrafamily bargaining between two partners that takes place within a three-period life cycle. Whereas during the first pre-family period human capital investments are made non-cooperatively by each individual, in subsequent periods, i.e. the family phases, time use decisions (in particular time devoted to housework as opposed to time spent in the labor market) are determined by the partners' maximization of the product of their gains from cooperation, i.e. Nash bargaining with separation as the threat point. In this model rational individuals not only tend to overinvest in human capital during their first period of life but also have an incentive to choose suboptimal time patterns at the beginning of the family phase should this happen to improve their bargaining position in the last period. This result is due to an asymmetry of the learning effects from market work versus housework and to the asymmetry of the marketability of the different labor skills, i.e. devoting time to gainful employment is assumed to yield higher gains of marketable human capital than spending time on household production. Unless binding long-term contracts can be made between the partners, individually rational behavior can lead to inefficient time allocation regarding housework and market work with the latter simultaneously serving as an insurance against the risk of divorce.

In the econometric implementation and analysis this strategic aspect of female labor force participation is estimated in a three-step procedure using data from the German Socio-economic Panel (GSOEP). Making use of the panel structure of these data, conflict payoffs that represent the divorce option to family life are estimated. Together with the predicted probabilities of divorce these "virtual conflict payoffs" are included as instrumental variables in a labor force participation equation. The explicit inclusion of the individual outside option to explain labor supply allows for the insurance aspects of intrafamily time allocation. The empirical results offer strong support to the bargaining argument based upon a strategic aspect of female employment.

The fifth chapter on household production casts light on the division of labor within German families, particularly the division of household tasks. The division of housework in Germany looks quite similar to what has been found with U.S. data. On average men perform 20% of a family's total housework and 30% of its child care, almost independent of specific household circumstances, i.e. in particular the employment status of their wives. In Chapter 5 the traditional time allocation theory is challenged by a non-cooperative approach to family bargaining that assumes a sequential structure of decision making within the household by means of a "dominance argument". Dominance is thereby defined as the ability to make irreversible decisions, particularly with regard to the use of time. The dominated partner has to take these decisions as given before making own decisions. The empirical evidence supporting the competing models is investigated using panel-econometric techniques. To investigate whether the division of housework among married German couples can be explained by factors identified in the competing theoretical approaches to intrafamily time allocation, a three-equation model is estimated using the GSOEP data. A mixed specification is applied that accounts for both effects of omitted individual-specific variables, fixed constants over time as well as random variables (fixed and random effects). The empirical results reveal that, even allowing for variables claimed by the traditional theory, gender-specific household activity is also influenced by the age difference between spouses. Age difference serves here as an indicator for a strategic advantage in family decision making for the older spouse. This finding supports the dominance argument that the "home chores gap" between husband and wife is greater the larger their age difference.

The third major time use, leisure, is the subject of Chapters 6 and 7. The question addressed is how leisure is distributed among family members and why generally men are observed to have more leisure time than women. In the German Time Budget Survey of 1991/92 for instance, the overall leisure gap between the sexes amounts to more than 20 minutes on an average day (Statistisches Bundesamt 1995). When it comes to working adults the gender-specific difference increases to over half an hour for full-timers. The greatest leisure gap, however, can be observed with households where both husband and wife hold a full-time employment and small children have to be looked after. For these couples the male partners have a full hour more per day than their spouses. Two explanations are proposed, one of a more general nature and one that particularly applies to couples with children. In Chapter 6, the only exclusively theoretical chapter, a non-cooperative bargaining model of intrafamily time allocation is developed that explains the leisure gap between husband and wife by means of sequential decision making (dominance argument). This model extends the framework presented in the preceding chapter by considering paid and unpaid work as two family public goods and leisure as the only private consumption good in the household. A first-mover advantage in family decision making will results in a higher share of household leisure time for the dominating party, the Stackelberg leader, with the size of the leisure gap depending on relative wages of husband and wife. In this model the leisure gap and the wage gap form a stable equilibrium of gender inequality. Chapter 7 focuses on the time use of working parents. Here the leisure gap between fathers and mothers is regarded as the outcome of an alternating offers game between family members. That is, both partners make a series of alternating offers to each other as how to distribute leisure time between themselves. Leisure is again assumed to be the only private consumption good in the household. A sharing rule for leisure is derived that is determined by gender-specific rates of time preference. This sharing rule is tested empirically with time use data from a German time use survey for 1991/92 controlling also for additional bargaining factors such as each spouses' income potential. While the results for married couples do not unambiguously support the bargaining hypothesis, for cohabiting couples there is empirical evidence consistent with family bargaining over the individual share of leisure time.

Chapter 8 is an assessment of the proposed models on intrafamily time allocation and the empirical evidence presented. In this concluding chapter the principal findings of the four studies are summarized and implications of the bargaining framework with regard to public policy are discussed. Finally the idea of an extension of the formal bargaining approach towards a qualitative bargaining framework will be sketched out.

2 Theories on intrafamily time allocation

2.1 The unitary model

There have been a variety of economic approaches that have attempted to explain the individual's choice of time use as well as the division of labor within a household setting. It was labor economist Jacob Mincer (1962) who first pointed out the importance of distinguishing between the times uses of market work, non-market work and leisure. The first systematic approach to a general theory of the allocation of time was made by Gary S. Becker (1965) in his pioneering contribution to what is now regarded as the New Home Economics. Becker's model was limited to the two-way decision between household production and market work. This approach was later extended by Reuben Gronau (1973, 1977) who then took account of the third time use leisure as opposed to home time in general. Both derive individual time use, particularly labor supply, from the maximization of a household utility function subject to budget and time constraints. In the first section of this chapter the household's time allocation problem will be introduced following the Gronau model although he himself did not explicitly set up a formal theory for the multi-person (family) case. The model presented here will for the most part follow Petra Radke's (1996) interpretation[3].

Keeping matters simple we will consider a two-person-household with a joint utility function. The family members are designated *f(emale)* and *m(ale)*. We assume this utility function to be twice differentiable and quasi-concave, with household utility depending on total consumption X and the family members' respective amounts of leisure time (respectively consumption time) L_f and L_m.

---

[3] Time allocation models with three time uses have among others also been presented by Althammer/Wenzler (1996), Assenmacher (1990), Graham/Green (1984) and Zimmermann (1985).

$$U = U(X, L_f, L_m)$$

Total consumption X is composed of goods and services that can either be purchased in the market (X_M) or produced at home (X_H). X_M and X_H are thereby assumed to be perfect substitutes for each other:

$$X = X_M + X_H$$

Male and female face time as well as budget constraints. Total available time, i.e. 24 hours per day deducting regeneration time, can be allocated among paid market work M, unpaid household work H and leisure L.

$$T = M_i + H_i + L_i \qquad i = m, f$$

In addition, total consumption is not to exceed the sum of individual labor incomes, the family's non-labor income and the amount of self-produced goods (the price of the market good is set to unity):

$$X \leq w_f M_f + w_m M_m + V + X_H$$

Home goods are produced using f's and m's time inputs (H_f and H_m). On the basis of the following household production function

$$X_H = Z(H_f + H_m),$$

that exhibits positive decreasing marginal productivity ($Z'>0$, $Z''<0$), and the assumption of non-satiation, the resulting budget restriction will have the form

$$w_f M_f + w_m M_m + V - X + Z(H_f + H_m) = 0 .$$

That is, total household consumption must not exceed male's plus female's wage incomes, non-wage income and household production.

Hence, the "unitary" household maximizes the following Lagrangian:

$$L(X, L_f, L_m, \lambda) =$$
$$U(X, L_f, L_m) + \lambda(w_f M_f + w_m M_m + V - X + Z(H_f + H_m))$$

Reformulating the first order conditions for an interior solution then yields the optimization conditions for female and male:

$$w_f = Z'(H_f + H_m) = \frac{U_{L_f}}{U_X}$$

$$w_m = Z'(H_f + H_m) = \frac{U_{L_m}}{U_X}$$

with $M_f>0$, $M_m>0$, $H_f>0$, $H_m>0$, $L_f>0$, $L_m>0$.

These conditions are only satisfied if $w_f = w_m$. That is, only with equal wages for female and male does an interior solution to the family time use problem exist where female and male allocate their time to all three time uses according to the equality of individual wage rate, marginal household productivity and marginal rate of substitution between leisure and consumption. If wages are not equated, if e.g. $w_f < w_m$ instead, specialization will result where at least one of the partners chooses only one or two time uses. The empirically most relevant specialization equilibria will occur in the following three cases:

1. $$w_f = \frac{U_{L_f}}{U_X} = Z' < \frac{U_{L_m}}{U_X} = w_m \quad \text{with } H_m = 0.$$

This case implies no male housework. That is, the man allocates his time among market work and leisure and supplies no housework, since his wage rate exceeds marginal household productivity. The woman performs all principal time uses.

2. $$w_f < \frac{U_{L_f}}{U_X} = Z' - \frac{U_{L_m}}{U_X} = w_m \quad \text{with } M_f = 0.$$

Specialization now turns out differently: Whereas the man does market, non-market and no work, the wage the woman could receive outside is too low for her to participate in the labor market at all. She thus specializes on household production and spends the remaining time taking leisure.

3. $$w_f < \frac{U_{L_f}}{U_X} = Z' < \frac{U_{L_m}}{U_X} = w_m \quad \text{with } H_m = 0 \text{ and } M_f = 0.$$

If the female wage rate falls short of and the male wage rate exceeds marginal household productivity the result will be complete specialization with solely female non-market work and male market work.

Further theoretical cases would include no household production performed by the household at all due to both female and male wages exceeding marginal productivity of housework, no (paid) labor supply by either family member due to low wages, or no leisure time.

Within this framework both spouses specialize according to their comparative advantages in the competing time uses. Analogous to trade theory the household serves as a market where the products are traded at prices that are determined by the partners' respective productivities in market work (wages) and in household production. Thus, a higher male wage rate automatically leads to the well-known gender-specific division of work. A wage differential in the labor market, as manifested in poorer promotion prospects or lower pay for women, will contribute to specialization, even with equal educational backgrounds of husband and wife. Furthermore, the mere ability of women to bear children as well as the complementarity between the bearing and rearing of children establishes a female comparative advantage in household activities, according to Becker (1981a: 21f). In this context the division of labor within families is seen as essentially biologically determined.

2.2 Under critique

If a family members' time use is derived from the maximization of a household utility function subject to pooled budget and time constraints, it still remains to be clarified just how such a joint utility function should come about; whether as a social welfare function of the sort proposed by Paul Samuelson (1956) or as the utility function of an altruistic "head of the household" as Becker suggested (in 1974b) or as some other aggregation of the individual utility functions of all family members. Samuelson was the first who postulated the existence of a household utility function based on distinct utilities of the family members. Since the members agree on a social welfare function, the family as a whole behaves as if it were maximizing this family welfare function. An optimal redistribution of income within the family would then occur according to the equality of all members' individual expenditures. Becker, on the contrary, proposed a model where the household utility function is that of an altruistic head of the household. As a benevolent dictator the head can thereby determine the intrafamily distribution of resources as long as he has the "last word" because he can then redistribute utility among family members according to his marginal utilities. This model of a paternal altruist is known as the "Rotten Kid Theorem"[4].

Apart from the question why individuals, who present themselves as egoistic and selfish decision making units in the outside market, should be driven by

---

[4] For a detailed discussion of the Rotten Kid Theorem see e.g. Hirshleifer (1977).

pure altruism within their families[5], the New Home Economics' break with the basic principle of methodological individualism seems critical, particularly from a neoclassical perspective (see among others McElroy/Horney 1981 and Chiappori 1988). By maximizing *one* household utility function the behavior of a whole family, represented by the head of the household, is optimized instead of that of an individual. Individuals are only characterized by distinct preferences as long as they are not married but household formation merges the family members' distinct preferences into a black box of a household utility function (Bourguignon/Chiappori 1992).

A second shortcoming concerns the disregard of the distributional aspects of time use decisions. According to Becker (1981a) the spouses-to-be anticipate all future household decisions when matching on the marriage market. Given complete information this implies that life-time-binding contracts on the distribution of marital gains are settled between matching partners at the moment of household formation. Consequently, distributional considerations will not play any role later. This requires not only the existence of binding contracts but also time-constant preferences that are not affected by changes in the family structure or other environmental circumstances. As Notburga Ott has noted (1998: 11) the Beckerian economic conception of the family does not provide a consistent theory, but rather a collection of single models that have been built for explaining quite distinct phenomena such as the occurrence of household formation and dissolution, intrahousehold time allocation, human capital investment or the timing of births.[6] Marriage and divorce are analyzed from the individual perspective, while during a marriage spouses' distinct preferences are merged into a joint household utility function. Distributional aspects are only considered when a household is formed or dissolved. Within a family, on the contrary, issues of distribution are ignored even when analyzing joint time use decisions.

A consequent application of the unitary framework results in a "vicious circle of economic rationality" that has been described by Ott (1993): Young women who are planning to have children eventually anticipate shorter and more discontinuous work lives as a consequence of the comparative advantages argument described above. As a result they decide to invest less in schooling and occupational training than similar young men. This leads to an observed wage differential between men and women according to their respective human capital endowments, again enhancing specialization gains from a gender-specific division of work within the household since it will now be the lower earning woman who interrupts gainful employment due to a baby break. Even if male and female applicants have the same educational

---

[5] For an elaboration of this point see Becker's "Altruism in the family and selfishness in the market place" (1981b).

[6] See Becker 1957, 1965, 1973, 1974a, 1974b, 1981a, 1981b and 1982.

status, employers are guided by this theoretically different work life of men and women, i.e. they statistically discriminate female applicants by favoring male employees or promoting male careers. The vicious circle comes full circle with the anticipation of the lower gains from female human capital investment and thereby contributing to the traditional household division of labor between women and men.

This static view, however, naturally ignores the long-run effects of human capital formation. Assume that the husband, by holding relatively continuous employment, steadily increases his human capital whereas his wife's marketable human capital remains unchanged over time or even decreases due to her specialization in housework. The husband's productivity advantage in doing market work is not constant, but is dynamically determined by the chosen division of labor. How high the gains from specialization will be, also varies with the actual household structure or the exact point in the family life cycle. Specialization gains are relatively greatest in households with small children with a high demand for household production, namely child care. However, whether a woman's complete specialization on household tasks would be efficient for households without or for those with older children is hardly obvious. As a consequence the Becker-Gronau time allocation framework appears only to be applicable to relatively brief periods determined by a household's actual demands. Given the unambiguous decline in average family size and the increase in life expectancy at the same time, this specific family period accounts for an ever decreasing proportion of an individual's lifetime, and hence family time allocation decisions (in particular female time use) are more likely to be affected by their long run consequences. With fading enforceability of the long-term marriage contract fewer women would be willing to give up gainful employment to specialize in household production, thereby sacrificing occupational human capital for marital- or family-specific human capital that is much less marketable.

Because the unitary model regards the household as a single decision-making unit, differing preferences of husband and wife as well as the existence of dominance or power relations within the household are ignored. This abstraction away from the influence of dominance or power relations on household decision-making leads a further criticism of the unitary model[7]. How such abstractions can result in misleading interpretations is illustrated by the following empirical example involving the discrimination faced by girls in South-Asian families: Mark Rosenzweig and Theodore P. Schultz (1982, 1984), using the unitary model, attributed the discrimination against girls,

[7] See Folbre (1994, 1997), Pollak (1994) and Woolley (1993). The feminist and marxian criticism of the unitary model also focuses on the importance of dominance and patriarchal structures for the gender-specific division of work. See Beblo/Soete (2000) for a brief review of the discussion.

with regard to investments in their nutrition, health and education, to the higher market returns to boys' labor in these societies. Favoring boys then appeared rational for parents in the sense of the human capital theory. Nancy Folbre (1984) objected that the seemingly rational discrimination could as well be interpreted within a bargaining framework with an asymmetric distribution of power between family members. Under the assumptions that women are better off with their daughters' help in the household, i.e. they prefer to invest more in girls, and that they have less power in household decision-making than their husbands, the observed discrimination and inequality within the household might rather be a reflection of the father's preferences than of household welfare maximization (Katz 1997).

The potential for misinterpretation of family realities through exclusive reliance on the unitary model has led to the desire for alternative approaches that regard the household as an arena of conflict and contest, as well as caring and cooperation, and that regard the observed primary responsibility for child care and housework as one that is socially imposed on women and not freely chosen (Seiz 1995).

2.3 Bargaining models

No doubt that these shortcomings together have led to growing challenges to the traditional approach by non-consensus or bargaining approaches to household behavior that treat the family members as distinct individuals having conflicting as well as common interests. Thus, in this second generation of home economic models, household behavior is seen as the result of bargaining that takes place between family members.[8]

In general bargaining models are characterized by the object of bargaining, the identification of the players' objectives, the set of feasible outcomes, the associated payoff for each player and the specification of rules by which outcomes are to be determined. With regard to household decisions the players, who are family members, bargain over the allocation of time, particularly the division of labor time and the distribution of leisure. Further objects for bargaining can be the distribution of resources and output, such as income and consumption goods as well as human capital investment. Both partners thereby seek to maximize their individual utilities. In contrast to the unitary model they are treated as sovereign decision-making units with their own optimization problems (which are of course interdependent). By explicitly

---

[8] For comprehensive surveys on bargaining models of household behavior see for instance Bergstrom (1996) and Lundberg/Pollak (1996). Lommerud (1997) discusses private-provision-of-public-goods games that are characterized by non-cooperation between family members.

addressing distributional considerations, assumptions of the Beckerian approach, such as the perfect predictibility of all decision parameters at the family formation stage as well as the possibility of life-time binding contracts, become obsolete for the most part. Having household members maximize their utilities according to their own tastes and preferences and within their individual restrictions offers the opportunity to account for gender-specific conditions, for instance in the labor market. The rules by which the players' outcomes are to be determined will differ according to the theoretic approach applied. For instance, game theory offers cooperative and non-cooperative bargaining approaches. Dynamic models can combine both cooperative as well as non-cooperative elements.

2.3.1 Cooperative bargaining

In common with the unitary model, cooperative bargaining models assume that individuals form a household when it is more beneficial to them than remaining alone. These gains can be the result of household formation implying a more efficient way to produce household goods than remaining single. Family members might also benefit from economies of scale in the sharing of goods. The gains accruing from household formation need to be distributed across members and it is the rule that governs this distribution that distinguishes bargaining models from the unitary models (Alderman et al. 1995).

In their seminal works Marilyn Manser and Murray Brown (1980) and Marjorie McElroy and Mary Jean Horney (1981) applied Nash cooperative bargaining theory to household decision making to analyze allocation and distribution between spouses. In these models the distribution of utility within the household is determined by the feasible consumption set of the two partners and their outside options[9] that is the utility each of them would obtain in the absence of agreement.

According to the axiomatic Nash solution[10] both partners act as if to maximize the product of their gains from cooperation $N=(U^m-C^m)(U^f-C^f)$ subject to a pooled household budget constraint. The cooperation gain arises from the difference between the individual utility when cooperating U^i and the alternatively attainable welfare level C^i. This alternatively achievable welfare level is also termed the *conflict payoff* or *threat point* since it represents the

---

9 The terms outside option, threat point and conflict payoff are used synonymously. They all indicate a person's best alternative to the bargaining outcome.

10 As Nash (1953, see also Harsanyi (1977)) showed, the Nash bargaining solution is uniquely characterized by the following four axioms: 1) Pareto efficiency, 2) symmetry, 3) invariance with regard to linear transformations and 4) independence from irrelevant alternatives.

threat potential against the partner in the case of disagreement and therefore clearly determines the bargaining outcome. The cooperative Nash solution replaces the Beckerian household utility function as a weighted average of the individual utility functions. The conflict payoffs thereby characterize the partners' relative weights. Any change in the relative conflict payoffs, e.g. an increase in income of one of the partners, will affect the household utility distribution in that spouse's favor.

Figure 2.1: Cooperative Nash bargaining solution

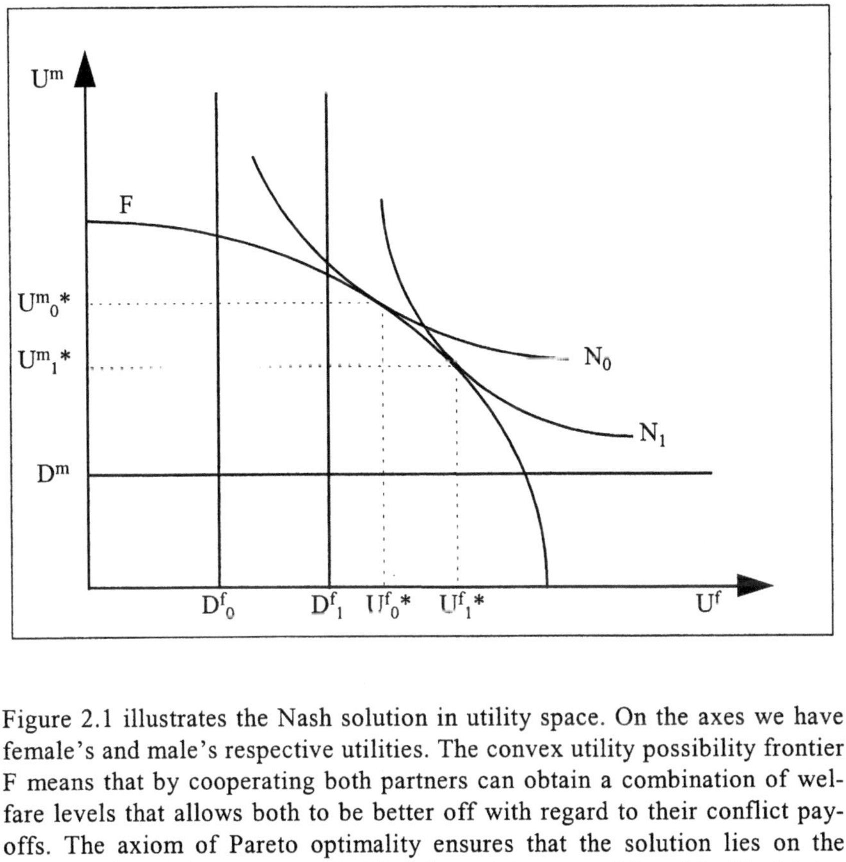

Figure 2.1 illustrates the Nash solution in utility space. On the axes we have female's and male's respective utilities. The convex utility possibility frontier F means that by cooperating both partners can obtain a combination of welfare levels that allows both to be better off with regard to their conflict payoffs. The axiom of Pareto optimality ensures that the solution lies on the frontier where it is tangent to the Nash bargaining curve N_0 or N_1. The higher a partner's threat point (compare D^f_0 and D^f_1) the higher will be his or her relative bargaining position and the resulting bargaining outcome (compare U^{f*}_0 to U^{f*}_1). Hence, intrahousehold allocation and distribution not only depends on prices and pooled family income but also on the determinants of the threat points, e.g. individual incomes.

Cooperative approaches can be divided into two groups with regard to the way they model the threat point. In bargaining models with *external* conflict payoffs, headed by Manser/Brown and McElroy/Horney, the threat point is the maximum level of utility attainable outside the marriage or the household. These we call divorce-threat models since the alternative to agreement consists of separation. In divorce-threat models the external alternative depends on the spouses' individual incomes and on extrahousehold environmental parameters (EEPs in McElroy's terminology (1990), or distribution factors in Browning et al. (1994)) that shift the threat point. EEPs could be the social network that provides support for child care or e.g. the chances of a better match on the marriage market, the legal structure for marriage and divorce and the conditioning of governmental transfers on marital status. Household behavior depends on these parameters as well, since the more favorable the individual outside option seems to be, the greater will be the share of the cooperation gain.

Frances Woolley (1988) and Shelly Lundberg and Robert Pollak (1993) proposed Nash bargaining models with *internal* conflict payoffs. In other words, in the case of disagreement both partners dissociate on non-cooperative behavior within the household. By staying in one household they still benefit from joint consumption of family public goods, such as a rented house or well-educated children, that are voluntarily provided by each spouse but they do not cooperate on the production of those goods anymore. As alternative to agreement Lundberg/Pollak suggested an inefficient non-cooperative equilibrium within marriage that is specified in terms of traditional gender roles. That is women and men provide gender-specific household goods. According to their model the traditional division of tasks - men being the breadwinners and women being responsible for the household sphere - might in fact be the solution of a non-cooperative equilibrium within marriage reflecting traditional gender roles rather then a specialization optimum as suggested by the New Home Economics. The separate-spheres model, in contrast to the divorce-threat model, also explains different equilibrium distributions in existing marriages implied by transfer payments to either of the partners, even if these do not affect the single state utilities. [11]

Cooperative bargaining games are based on the assumptions of free communication between the players, symmetry of information and of voice, i.e. access to bargaining, and the existence of free and binding contracts. With respect to the latter assumption Nash bargaining does not differ much from the Beckerian time allocation approach: Once a woman has agreed to a traditional division of labor and her husband has agreed to provide a financial compensation for her household production, this contract is assumed to be

[11] The dynamic Konrad-Lommerud model (1996) to be discussed later also assumes non-cooperative behavior as the partners' threat points.

irreversible and effective until the end of marriage. Re-bargaining does not occur in this framework although it might be attractive for the husband if - after a couple of years - the wife has decreased opportunities on the labor market and therefore faces a distinctly less favorable bargaining position than he does. Only a strong emotional tie or institutional structures will then ensure that the terms of the contract are still met. Otherwise the time inconsistency between the wife's cooperative decision (to give up her job and to stay home with the children) and the husband's cooperative behavior (to ensure a fixed share of utility) runs the risk of a breach of contract due to the incentives described.

Another crucial assumption of cooperative game theory is the Pareto efficiency of all outcomes. According to this assumption bargaining guarantees intrafamily time allocation and distribution of resources where no family member's position could be improved without diminishing another member's welfare.

This assumption is the starting point of another kind of non-consensus model developed by Pierre-André Chiappori (1988, 1992). He proposes an alternative model of household behavior, namely the collective model, that assumes household allocations to be Pareto optimal but avoids specifying any particular bargaining game or collective decision process. Chiappori justifies the assumption of Pareto efficiency with the repeated-game character of household decisions so that cooperation emerges as a long-term equilibrium of repeated non-cooperative frameworks (Browning/Chiappori 1998).

A very intuitive property of this class of cooperative models is the sharing rule interpretation (Bourguignon/Chiappori 1992, Chiappori 1997). Once a household has decided on the expenditures for public goods, PX, the members agree on the share of the remaining income, $y - PX$, each of them is allowed to spend. The sharing rule ϕ may depend on prices and income. In addition it is determined by the EEPs mentioned above: one partner receives $\phi(p,P,y,EEPs)$ and the other one receives $y\text{-}PX\text{-}\phi(p,P,y,EEPs)$[12]. The sharing rule reflects the outcome of the decision process and each partner maximizes his or her utility, subject to the budget constraint thus defined. That is, if $x^A(p,P,y,EEPs)$, $x^B(p,P,y,EEPs)$ and $X(p,P,y,EEPs)$ is the chosen consumption

[12] Whether one assumes the sharing rule to be exogenously given or rather endogenously determined depends on the cultural background of the families to be analyzed. In Arabic countries, for instance, the sharing rule might well be taken as given through say the legal status of women, whereas in Western developed countries the extent to which the sharing can be influenced is certainly much higher. But even with the latter environment are there still exogenous factors (such as age) that affect the division of resources by gender, as shown in the study on leisure time presented in Chapter 7.

bundle, then there exists a sharing rule $\phi(p,P,y,EEPs)$ such that (Bourguignon et al. 1993, Chiappori 1997):

$x^A(p,P,y,EEPs)$ is the solution of $max\ U^A(x^A,X)$, subject to $p^Ax^A = \phi(p,P,y,EEPs)$ and $x^B(p,P,y,EEPs)$ is the solution of $max\ U^B(x^B,X)$, subject to $p^Bx^B = y - PX - \phi(p,P,y,EEPs)$.

Another empirically appealing property of the sharing rule is that, up to a constant, it can easily be recovered from private consumption data of an exclusive good (for instance leisure) (Browning et al. 1994). If one good is assignable it can directly be observed how exogenous changes in the economic environment affect the spouse's consumption. Such consumption data is sufficient for recovering the entire decision process, since the pattern of the sharing rule variation in response to say changes in each partner's income can be identified. Only the initial level of the sharing rule remains unknown (Chiappori 1997). A shortcoming of the collective approach, however, is the neglect of housework as a distinct time use. Patricia Apps and Ray Rees (1997) extend Chiappori's results by including household production. They show that the retrievability of the partial derivatives of the sharing rule does not continue to hold in this extended setting unless further restrictions on preferences and technology are imposed.

The distribution of leisure within a household, or in other words, family bargaining on how much free time each spouse can dispose of, characterizes a special case of the sharing rule concept. In Chapter 7 an application of the sharing rule concept to the distribution of leisure among spouses is presented where the sharing rule is estimated as a linear representation of the partner's rates of time preference and other bargaining factors.

Free communication, symmetry and the existence of binding contracts between partners might be suitable assumptions to analyze a household's day-to-day decision problems (such as "Who will take out the garbage?") because these may well have repeated-game character. However, due to their far-reaching impact on future income potentials, symmetry and binding contracts in particular are not always reasonable to impose. The suitability of these assumptions might especially be doubted with regard to fundamental and life-determining questions like giving up one's gainful employment or deciding to have a child. From a dynamic perspective, also Pareto efficiency seems problematic since Pareto efficient specialization gains again can only be guaranteed through binding long-term contracts between the partners[13].

---

[13] For an illustration see Ott (1992).

2.3.2 Non-cooperative bargaining

Non-cooperative bargaining games do not require assuming symmetric information nor Pareto-efficient outcomes. The players cannot communicate or make binding agreements. In contrast to the cooperative framework, non-cooperative games explicitly specify a bargaining process and thereby model strategic behavior of the individuals involved. Although one partner cannot coordinate his or her choices with the other, individual utility maximization depends on the decisions made by one's partner, for instance due to household public goods that only have to be produced by one partner but can then be consumed by both. Non-cooperation might be characterized by coordination problems, regarding e.g. the coordination of career choices (Lommerud 1997), it might be formulated as a principal-agent model or it might fall into the category of conflicting objectives.

The Separate-spheres bargaining model of Lundberg/Pollak (1993), that has already been listed as a cooperative bargaining game with internal conflict payoffs above, can also be interpreted as an example of a coordination game on the provision of two household public goods. Analogous to the original "battle-of-the-sexes" game it has two Nash equilibria: one in which the wife supplies one good and the husband contributes the other one and another with reversed provider roles. Lundberg and Pollak (1994: 136) argue that the "choice between these equilibria is likely to be sensitive to history and culture". A corner solution to this public goods provision might result where complete gender specialization corresponds to social norms and traditional assignment of responsibilities. Due to the corner solution distribution within the household clearly depends on the individual resources of husband and wife. Another coordination model of the sexual division of labor is proposed by Gillian Hadfield (1999). There, specialization results from coordinated human capital investments made in order to secure a compatible match on the marriage market. A particular division of labor, that predicts particular tasks for women and men is assumed to depend on institutional and historical facts, just as in the former model. Hadfield employs a joint utility function of the household to derive the theoretical results, though.

When modeling intrahousehold decision-making by means of the principal-agent framework one assumes the family to be characterized by an employer-employee relationship where only one partner owns the productive wealth (land, money). This type of model has been used to explain the intrafamily division of labor in West-Africa, where men as principals have ownership of land-use rights and working capital and can induce their wives as agents to work on their fields by offering them a welfare level at least slightly above their reservation utility. Under these economic and social constraints the non-cooperative treatment of household decision making seems appropriate, because women and men act economically independent from each other.

Moreover the principal-agent framework offers the possibility to endogenize intrahousehold power by considering women's options as highly constrained if men monopolize access to productive resources.

In models of conflicting objectives family members try to free-ride on the public-good provision of the others (Leuthold 1968; Konrad/Lommerud 1995). In this type of non-cooperative household both partners decide on their time allocation and their provision of the family public good. They choose between a private consumption good purchased by income-generating employment and a public consumption good produced by unpaid labor. Whether they act simultaneously in a Cournot-Nash framework taking their partner's behavior as given, as in the Konrad-Lommerud model, or whether they choose their actions in a pre-specified order depends on the consideration of dominance in these models.

Kristian Bolin (1996, 1997) and Susan Fleck (1996) for example consider dominance or power within a family as the cause of asymmetric decision-making between partners and explain unequal division of family work as the outcome of a Stackelberg game between the spouses[14]. Assuming that the husband holds the dominant part he is the Stackelberg leader who can decide on his time allocation first. He acts, whereas his wife can only react, given his time use and his contribution to the household public good. Dominance reveals a first-mover advantage of the dominating spouse with regard to household decision-making. Apart from any comparative advantages, dominance within a family leads to a specialization in paid labor of the dominating spouse and the provision of the family good by the dominated spouse. Furthermore it further increases the utility of the dominating spouse and decreases the other spouse's welfare since paid labor is the only income- and thus private-consumption-good-generating source.

In Chapter 5 the impact of dominance on the division of household work will be investigated empirically with the Stackelberg advantage measured by the age difference between spouses. The studies of Chapter 6 and 7 also apply non-cooperative bargaining between family members. There the reviewed literature will be extended by treating market work and housework as two family public goods. Hence, spouses will be seen to bargain on the distribution of leisure time as it is assumed to constitute the only private good.

---

[14] In this context the term *dominance* stands for the ability to make irreversible decisions and to force the partner to take these decisions as given. In Fleck (1996) to dominate even means to oppose to the dominated partner's choice.

2.3.3 Dynamic models

Dynamic models combine the cooperative Nash-bargaining framework with the strategic component of non-cooperative games. They model the dynamic impacts of a time use decision on human capital formation. Notburga Ott (1992), Kai Konrad and Kjell Erik Lommerud (1996) and Robin Wells and Maria Maher (1996) account for strategic behavior within the family in the form of sequential non-cooperation. These papers take account of intertemporal dependencies of household decisions in proposing dynamic bargaining models with subgame consistency. In this setting the partners' outside options are not given exogenously any more, instead they are endogenously determined by the preceding period's time allocation. An individual's decision to invest in education or to supply labor is made allowing for the accompanying impact on his or her future conflict payoff. The partners' relative bargaining powers therefore directly depend on past time use decisions and the resulting human capital accumulation. Sequential non-cooperation does not allow to sign binding contracts between the periods. If for example a woman gives up gainful employment due to the birth of a child, this will typically result in lower career prospects accompanied by weaker bargaining power relative to her permanently employed spouse. As a result, rational individuals will not be willing to enter such agreements with regard to their future bargaining position even though this might be the most efficient way to allocate family time for a certain period in the family life cycle (e.g. when infants have to be taken care of).

The dynamic framework seems to be most appropriate for explaining labor force participation of many women who not only consider actual wage income but also the human capital aspect of job experience as well as their future bargaining power within the household when making time use decisions. Educational investments or labor supply then become strategic variables since they affect future bargaining power via the accumulation of human capital. The strategic aspect of supplying labor is elaborated in Chapter 4 where female employment is modeled in a dynamic framework and the impact of bargaining considerations on time use is investigated empirically.

2.3.4 Summing up

In general we can say that static cooperative bargaining models of the family rather apply to household's day-to-day decision because these may well be assumed to have repeated-game character. Time use decisions that have long-run consequences are best modeled within a dynamic framework that allows for sequential non-cooperation between partners. This way the problem of time inconsistency in cooperative behavior of wife and husband can be considered, as e.g. associated with the decision whether to have a baby or not and the question of who will be the one to quit paid employment. A dynamic bargaining model will be applied to the analysis of female labor force participation in Chapter 4.

Consumption decisions might be most appropriately modeled in a non-cooperative bargaining setting. For example the distribution of leisure as one consumption good can be assumed to result from non-cooperative bargaining between spouses. This aspect will be further investigated in Chapters 6 and 7.

Those models that view the household as being a single decision-making unit can lead to misinterpretations of the long reach of public interventions. Consider for example a policy reform that imposes a payroll tax on every wage earner in order to raise the child benefit paid to mothers. Since this additional tax burden is mostly born by male earners the reform implies a substantial reallocation of income within the household although total income might not even have changed for the family as a whole. Due to joint utility maximization subject to a pooled budget constraint the unitary framework would not predict any changes in family behavior in this case. Bargaining approaches, on the contrary, take into consideration the recipient of the income payment and the impact on household members' bargaining powers. According to the specific bargaining model applied we would expect a different utility distribution within the household as the result of a variation of the tax-transfer system. For this reason it is important to test how resources are actually allocated and how control over resources influences distribution within households. In other words, it is important to test whether the unitary model or the bargaining approaches provide better predictions with regard to family behavior. A review of some examples of the empirical literature for bargaining models of the household is given in the next chapter.

3 Empirical evidence on intrafamily time allocation

3.1 Introduction

Whether intrahousehold time allocation, respectively resource allocation, is determined by joint utility maximization of the household or by cooperative or non-cooperative bargaining between family members turns out to be critical to our interpretation of the changing patterns of women and men's time use, in particular with respect to increasing female employment. It is also critical to our understanding of the impact of welfare reforms on the behavior and economic welfare of different household members and it has specifically different implications for social policy measures and the design of the tax-transfer system. Each of the frameworks described in the previous chapter is based on a different set of assumptions and makes different predictions about the distribution of resources within households. In order to select the most appropriate model for a particular situation, the validity of the prevailing assumptions have to be tested against the data. Another question to be asked would be whether the outcomes that we observe are consistent with the framework and predictions of the prevailing model (Doss 1996).

As outlined in the previous chapter, the joint utility model is based on the assumption of income pooling between family members and on the presumption of Pareto efficient outcomes within the household. A third restriction is the equality between Slutsky cross-substitution effects. Transferring this property of consumption theory to the household setting implies that an income-compensated rise of the first spouse's wage should have the same effect on the second spouse's labor supply as the second spouse's wage increase has on the labor supply of the first. A rejection of any of these assumptions implies a rejection of the unitary model. Whereas the rejection of the income pooling hypothesis and the Slutsky symmetry assumption would still be consistent with Chiappori's collective framework or cooperative bargaining models, both approaches critically assume Pareto optimal allocations within the household. Thus, any empirical analysis revealing inefficient outcomes with regard to intrahousehold resource allocation and distribution of goods provides evidence against the unitary as well as the collective and the cooperative model. Only non-cooperative and dynamic bargaining models that allow for sequential non-cooperation would be consistent with a rejection of Pareto efficiency. In the following, recent empirical studies are reviewed that test the income pooling hypothesis, the Slutsky symmetry restrictions and Pareto efficiency within the household[1]. In addition, the empirical relationship between household behavior and variations in extrahousehold environmental parameters (EEP) is investigated. Finally the contribution of economic analysis to the impact of the balance of power within a family on observed household outcomes will be discussed.

3.2 Testing for unitary income pooling

According to the income pooling restriction, the marginal value of income should be equalized across family members. This assumption implies that for the consumption decision it should not matter who receives or controls income, since if all income is pooled and serves as a budget constraint to the maximization of a single utility function, only total family income will affect household demand. In fact "much of the empirical work on intrahousehold resource allocation uses the overall pattern of household expenditure data as a proxy." (Doss 1996: 1601). Nevertheless if household expenditure differs depending on who earns the income or, what is even more important from the perspective of the policy maker, who receives the transfer payment, we can still conclude that the allocation of resources within the household has changed, even though we do not observe exactly who obtains what. If the pooling hypothesis were accurate this would imply the ineffectiveness of targeted transfer policies, since transfer payments that attempted to redistribute income to particular family members would be neutralized by the intrafamily allocation process (Lundberg/Pollak/Wales 1997). In bargaining models, on the contrary, income received by different family members would affect consumption and time use decisions differently through changes in relative bargaining powers.

As labor earnings are directly linked to the number of hours gainfully employed, they are clearly endogenous with respect to allocation decisions, since working hours are one of the main choice variables when modeling household behavior. In terms of individual wage income, it is therefore difficult to distinguish between the unitary and the bargaining approaches. Al-

[1] Comprehensive surveys on empirical evidence of intrahousehold resource allocation are among others provided by Alderman et al. (1995), Behrman (1997), Doss (1996), Hoddinott et al. (1997) and Strauss/Thomas (1996).

though in the unitary model allocations are solely based on marginal productivity and in the bargaining framework they are additionally driven by the family members' threat potentials, as for the impact of a change in wage income both are observationally equivalent (Doss 1996). Whereas in the unitary model a rise in women's wages induces an increase in female labor force participation through the reallocation of time within households, the cooperative setting additionally predicts that women renegotiate the gains from marriage on the basis of this new earnings opportunity (Hoddinott et al. 1997). Thus, the same outcome, higher women's labor supply or a substitution of household work with market goods, is predicted by both approaches, even though to a different extent and for different reasons.

The analysis of changes in non-labor income, that do not alter family members' marginal productivities but do affect their bargaining positions, provides a more accurate means of testing the income pooling assumption. The result could be a variation in a household's consumption pattern or labor supply pattern. Let us focus on investigations on the consumption pattern first.

In Duncan Thomas (1990, 1993) the equality of parental income effects on family nutrition in Brazil is rejected. Using Brazilian survey data he finds that nonlabor income under the control of the mother has a bigger effect on family's health and child survival probabilities than father's income. In later papers[16] further evidence against the pooling hypothesis is provided: Nonlabor income controlled by women is associated with larger increases of the household budget share being devoted to human capital and leisure. Furthermore it has a positive impact on the health of daughters but not on sons' health. Household expenditure patterns are furthermore determined by the percentage of assets owned by women, as Cheryl Doss (1996) concludes for Ghana.

Empirical tests on the assumptions of the unitary model have not been confined to developing countries. Also in highly developed states has it been investigated whether policy changes would affect the intrahousehold allocation of resources through a shift in individual nonlabor incomes. Studies on Canadian household expenditure data[17] show that couples (with no children) do *not* pool their income and, thus, "incomes affect outcomes" (Browning et al. 1994: 1067). Martin Browning and co-authors for instance analyze clothing demands of married couples where both spouses work full-time. This way they justify their treatment of labor supply as exogenously given. Under some additional assumptions (namely efficiency, caring preferences and the assign-

---

[16] See Thomas/Chen (1994) on Taiwan, Thomas (1994) on the U.S., Brazil and Ghana and Thomas (1997) on Brazil.

[17] Conducted among others by Browning and co-authors (1994) and Browning/Chiappori (1998).

ability of clothing) the authors can identify how intrahousehold sharing is affected, among other factors, by individual incomes. In a reproduction of this test on French household data, income pooling is also rejected for French full-time working couples (Bourguignon et al. 1993). In these studies the share of each spouse's income matters for the household consumption pattern.

Shelly Lundberg, Robert Pollak and Terence Wales (1997) present a test of the pooling hypothesis based on a "natural experiment" provided by a change in the United Kingdom child benefit scheme in the late 1970s. This policy change that transferred the benefit from a tax deduction of the father to a substantial child allowance to the mother resulted in an increase of expenditures on women's and children's goods relative to men's goods. The authors conclude that, in contrast to the pooling hypothesis, who receives and controls income in the household significantly affects the family expenditure pattern. In accordance with the findings for developing countries Lundberg/Pollak/Wales conclude that children do better when their mothers control a larger fraction of family resources (1997: 479).

Instead of looking at expenditure data, Frances Woolley (1996) examines the flow of tax benefits, including child benefits, through the household. To answer the question of whether the tax recipient matters, she investigates the financial management of Canadian families and finds a higher probability of a woman's income to be deposited into her own account (six times higher than with income received by the male) and a child tax benefit to be saved. 33 percent of child tax benefits are saved whereas only 15-21 percent of either source of employment income go into a savings account, suggesting some sort of earmarking of the child tax benefit. No information is given on compensating behavior, though. We might expect other income sources to flow to other purposes (and other family members) as a reaction to the tax receipt.

As an alternative line the implications of the unitary model for household time use decisions, particularly labor supply and the demand for leisure can be tested: Mary Jean Horney and Marjorie McElroy (1988) present an empirical application of their Nash bargaining model of household decision making using U.S. National Longitudinal Survey data. Using a linear expenditure system for three goods (male labor supply, female labor supply and expenditures on a composite commodity), they show that labor supply is significantly determined by individual nonwage income. However, differences in female and male income effects are only significant for the husband's labor supply equation. In comparison, Theodore Paul Schultz (1990) finds differential effects of male and female nonlabor income on *female* labor supply and fertility in Thailand. By estimating multi-sector labor supply equations for men and women in Brazil, Jill Tiefenthaler (1999) discovers different effects of own and spousal nonwage income. Marilyn Manser and Murray Brown (1979) who estimate a system of three household demand equations for female leisure, male leisure and a composite commodity, have rejected equal effects of husband's and wife's unearned income on household behavior as well. A recent study for Italy investigates the impact male income has on leisure demands as opposed to the female income effect (Del Boca 1997). With household data of the Bank of Italy's Survey the equality of non-labor income effects is rejected. For families with pre-school children, however, income pooling cannot be rejected.

Richard Blundell et al. (1998) use a collective framework to analyze family labor supply of British couples, allowing for the possibility that one or both partners do not work. With data from the UK Family Expenditure Survey they decisively reject the income restriction of the unitary model.

Complementing the earlier work by Lundberg/Pollak/Wales (1997) Ian Walker and Yu Zhu (1999) investigate the impact of the exogeneous change in child benefit payments in the UK in the late 1970s on mothers' and fathers' labor supplies. They find a reduction in hours for both mothers and fathers that does not point to a strong rejection of the unitary model.

Most of the studies cited suggest that unearned income as an exogenous variable affects the bargaining power of men and women in a cooperative setting. They provide evidence for rejecting the unitary model, since, if household behavior depends on who has control over income, family members are not acting as though they completely pool their income or as if they have identical preferences.

It should be noted, however, that problems arise with the interpretation of these results should the measure of nonlabor income under investigation not be exogenous to household behavior (Behrman 1997). As soon as nonearned incomes, e.g. pensions or property income from savings, are related to past wages or productivity, they capture preferences with regard to time use just as wage income does. This is why Lundberg/Pollak/Wales' (1997) analysis of the UK policy change that distributed income from husbands to wives provided important new evidence against the income pooling hypothesis. Since child benefits are unlikely to be related to prices and preferences regarding time use decisions, a shift in the child allowance scheme can be unambiguously interpreted as an exogenous shock to family members' incomes.

3.3 Testing for Slutsky symmetry

Although not for income pooling, the family members' earned wage incomes can be subject to alternative tests of the unitary model. For example, it can be tested whether the effect an income-compensated increase in a man's wage has on his partner's labor supply is identical to the effect of an income-compensated increase in the woman's wage on her spouse's labor supply.

Several studies have rejected the equality of these cross-substitution effects (see e.g. Killingsworth 1983). Interestingly, responses to wage changes seem to be subject to race differences: As Horney/McElroy (1988) find, white husbands and wives in the U.S. have differing labor elasticities with respect to changes in own and spouses' wage rates, while nonwhites' responses are symmetric.

Children also make a difference here: Estimating labor supply functions for married men and women in a dynamic simultaneous equations system, Lundberg (1988) even rejects the hypothesis that the labor supply of husbands and wives without pre-school children is jointly determined at all. More recent analyses provide further evidence against a symmetry of the Slutsky matrix[18]. Bernard Fortin and Guy Lacroix (1997), using Canadian data on working couples, reject Slutsky symmetry, (as well as the income pooling hypothesis) for most of the subgroups. At the same time, households with pre-school children do not seem to behave consistent with the collective approach. The empirical evidence presented by Fortin/Lacroix thus suggests that the collective model is inadequate in the case of young couples with pre-school children, as Maria Concetta Chiuri (1997) puts it. She extends the framework to include young children. When examining the labor supply decisions of Italian households who use formal child care, Chiuri finds evidence for the extended version of the collective model. She also rejects the restrictions imposed by the Slutsky's symmetry condition.

Benjamin Senauer (1990) discusses three studies on the value of women's time and intrahousehold food allocation in Sri Lanka and the Philippines, where the value of time is measured by the woman's estimated wage rate. Children's nutritional status as well as mother's and children's relative calorie allocation improved with the mother's increasing education level and wage rate. The Philippine father's wage, on the contrary, had a negative impact on his children's long-run nutritional status.

Overall, we can conclude that cross-substitution effects are not symmetric within households. Thus the standard restriction from consumer demand does not continue to hold for the multiple-person case, meaning that joint utility maximization does not seem to be an appropriate way for treating family decision problems.

3.4 Testing for Pareto efficiency

Pareto efficiency within household decision making is the basic assumption not only of the unitary but also the cooperative bargaining model and the

---

[18] See for example Blundell et al. (1993), Browning/Meghir (1991) and Browning/Chiappori (1998).

collective approach as the overruling framework. Two aspects of Pareto efficiency can be tested. First, if the ratio of income effects is constant across all pairs of goods, that is if all individuals face equal marginal utility, *consumption goods* are allocated Pareto efficiently within the household. Second, if the ratio of marginal productivities is constant across all production activities, that is if resources yield equal marginal productivities, *time* is allocated Pareto efficiently within the household (Doss 1996).

With respect to the first aspect Duncan Thomas and Chien-L. Chen (1994), using Taiwanese household budget data, show that the ratio of male to female income effects is indeed equated across all commodities. They find resource allocations to be Pareto efficient. French consumption data also seem consistent with this assumption and thus with the collective framework. According to Francois Bourguignon et al. (1993) full-time working couples consume such that marginal utility is the same across partners.

As for the production aspect, on the contrary, Christopher Udry (1996) finds that in Burkina Faso plots controlled by women are farmed less labor intensively than those controlled by men within the same household. Yields are 30 percent lower for female cultivators. This contradicts the Pareto efficiency of resource allocation within the household respectively across each household's plots. The estimation results rather suggest an increase of total output by reallocating factors between men's and women's plots or by reallocating land. Christine Jones' (1983) study also detects allocative inefficiencies in women's labor on rice production in North Cameroon: only those married women who receive high enough financial compensations from their husbands spend as much time cultivating rice as for instance widows do. The remaining women's households are allocatively inefficient compared to widows' households, suggesting that they are holding out for higher compensation.

In summary, no conclusive answer has been given as to the appropriateness of the Pareto efficiency assumption yet. To date the least we can say is that the assumption of a Pareto optimal allocation of consumption goods across household members has not been rejected in studies on more developed countries. This literature suggests that although the unitary model may be too restrictive, households do behave Pareto efficiently.

Whereas a rejection of Pareto efficiency would imply a denial of the collective framework, including the unitary and the cooperative bargaining model as special cases, it does not challenge a non-cooperative approach, be it the non-cooperative fall back of a Nash bargaining model or a non-cooperative game between family members. On the contrary, the non-cooperative as well as the dynamic bargaining framework explicitly allow for Prisoner's dilemma-like situations where total outcome and each family member's outcome could be increased if binding long-term contracts on intrafamily allocation and distribution existed. There are, however, empirical problems in distinguishing between a static non-cooperative model and a dynamic bargaining model with sequential non-cooperation, since both approaches take account of Pareto inefficient time allocation (for instance when neither of the partners is willing to specialize on child care even if this might be a Pareto optimal choice for a given short time period). One starting point to differentiate between the two models would be an analysis of the impact of a threat point variation on time use behavior. While in the standard non-cooperative approach changes in bargaining positions are only predicted with a variation of the present outside option, household decisions in the dynamic framework are also determined by dynamic variations of the individual threat point levels.

3.5 Testing for the impact of EEPs and decision-making power

It was McElroy (1990) who first suggested including "extrahousehold environmental parameters" (EEPs) in a nested testing of the Nash and the traditional model. EEPs as indices of the control over resources outside the family (e.g. social networks or chances on the remarriage market) are determinants of the threat points. In other words, they serve as shifters of the threat points and as such help to explain time allocation in general and labor supply in particular. Since in the unitary model the opportunity costs of being married are not relevant, a statistical link between EEPs and intrahousehold allocation would provide evidence to reject its restrictions.

Examples of EEPs include a country's legal structure governing marriage and divorce or the conditioning of governmental transfers on marital status. As a consequence, a considerable extent of research has been focussed on the impact of divorce laws and marital-property laws on household behavior. Paul S. Carlin (1991) investigated the effect of EEP variations on U.S.-American couples' time use decisions. Interestingly, women living in states with more generous divorce settlements were found to invest more in their human capital by increasing education and working time at the expense of home production and leisure. Using 1979 U.S. data both H. Elizabeth Peters (1986) and Allen M. Parkman (1992) conclude that the introduction of unilateral divorce has increased the labor force participation rate of married women. Whereas Peters attributes this response to the lack of compensation for marriage-specific investment at divorce creating an incentive for wives to enter the labor force and increase their marketable capital, Parkman reasons with the lack of compensation for wives' reduced human capital considering the dynamic effects of human capital depreciation for married women. He finds a greater effect of unilateral divorce on the labor supply of younger and better educated women who would experience larger reductions in their future earning capacity if labor force participation were to be reduced. Jeffrey

Gray's (1998) results reveal a responsiveness of the labor-supply behavior of U.S.-American wives' especially to divorce laws that effectively redistribute property rights[19].

Taking data on seven countries from the Luxembourg Income Study Shelley Phipps and Peter Burton (1995) conduct empirical tests of the impact of social/institutional factors on behavior within marriage. Their empirical results indicate "that the labor-force participation of married women is significantly influenced by the institutions of the countries in which they live. For example, higher social transfers for single women or higher levels of child support for single mothers are observed to reduce levels of labor-force participation of married women, other things equal." (Phipps/Burton 1995: 168). An increase of single women's equivalent social transfers (divided by median income) by one unit or an increase of standardized child support received by single mothers by one-and-a-half units is associated with a two-percent drop in married women's participation in the labor market. Phipps/Burton also find a significantly positive relation between the probability of divorce within a country and the labor force participation of currently married women.

Pierre-Andre Chiappori, Bernard Fortin and Guy Lacroix (1997) define variables that influence the decision process but that are exogenous with respect to preferences and the joint consumption set as "distribution factors". These distribution factors comprise personal income variables as well as EEPs. The authors introduce the sex ratio as a distribution factor in a parametric model of household labor supply. Since for instance a high proportion of women in the population implies a scarcity of men in the marriage market, the sex ratio is an EEP that affects spouses' opportunities outside marriage and thereby influences their bargaining positions. With data from the Panel Study of Income Dynamics the authors can identify the intrahousehold sharing rule as a function of wages, nonlabor income and the sex ratio. The latter significantly affects labor supply behavior, in that the higher the proportion of women the more female and the less male labor supply, hence the lower female and the higher male leisure time results[20].

While the sociological literature has a long-standing tradition in the consideration of the impact of the power balance in a family on household outcomes, economists have only recently begun to analyze household behavior in the presence of power differentials. One example is the work of Simone Dobbelsteen and Peter Kooreman (1997) who argue that, if "the distribution of power between partners is reflected in the extent to which both partners'

---

[19] For further discussion of the empirical literature on the relation between divorce laws and female labor force participation see the empirical part of Chapter 4.

[20] Manser/Brown (1979) found similar effects when including search costs and expectations in the marriage market, measured by the ratio of single female to single males, in their estimation of a household demand system.

preferences are weighted in the final household decision: the most powerful spouse will be better able to realize his/her preferences." (1997: 345f). With British data on households' financial management and financial decision-making they test the unitary model and a cooperative Nash bargaining model as competing explanations of how finances are organized within a family. Whereas in the first model the division of responsibilities should be determined by an efficient allocation of both partners' time to market work, financial management and leisure, in the second model it is assumed to be a reflection of bargaining power. For strategic control aspects of financial management (e.g. the question who has the final say in big financial decisions) the power argument is found to dominate the efficiency argument. The empirical results show that only with regard to executive management activities, that is everyday household spending, efficiency considerations appear to play a larger role.

Another way of quantifying power in household distribution is proposed by Susan Fleck (1996) who investigates whether the estimation of married women's labor force participation in Honduras can be improved by including a measure of the probability of men's domination as a reflection of social norms. The finding is a significantly negative effect of the husband's domination on the wife's labor supply. Alternatively, Kristian Bolin (1996) suggests taking the age difference between husband and wife as a proxy for dominance and testing whether this difference affects female labor supply. However, his hypothesis of dominance is not accepted with Swedish data.

In an empirical application of a fertility model Notburga Ott (1992) investigates whether the probability of practicing birth control is linked with changes in intrafamily power relations. She proposes a function of the spouses' wage ratio as an indicator variable for symmetry in their bargaining positions. The finding is that working couples with a more symmetrical situation and occupational opportunities for the wife are more likely to practice birth control. For non-working women this probability increases with their earnings potential. The no-child solution is interpreted as a Prisoner's dilemma situation of non-cooperative behavior between spouses that is more likely to apply to symmetric bargaining positions. In this case a baby break would imply a substantial decrease in female relative bargaining power.

In summarizing we can conclude that substantial evidence has been gathered against the income pooling hypothesis and the assumption of symmetric cross-substitution effects. There are ambiguous results as to the existence of Pareto efficient outcomes within the household, though. Since a rejection of any of these assumptions implies a rejection of the unitary model, we would be well advised to seriously consider alternative models and not rely exclusively, if at all, on the joint utility maximizing framework for modeling family time use behavior. Nevertheless, the evidence does not support any particular bargaining model. As collective and cooperative bargaining models hinge on the assumption of Pareto efficiency, we cannot conclusively answer the question of whether they provide an adequate framework for the outcomes that we observe. With respect to the evidence on the impact of EEP-variations and power relations, we can nonetheless unambiguously agree on the important role of individual bargaining positions for the outcome of family decision making.

Given the differing results for families with and without children with regard to the rejection of income pooling and Slutsky symmetry, it seems that the extent to which the family members' distinct incomes affect household expenditures or intrafamily time allocation depends on household composition and the stage of the life cycle. Each stage might be best characterized by a particular bargaining game between family members based on a specific set of assumptions. Which bargaining framework to choose therefore crucially depends on the kind of policy conclusion that needs to be drawn from the analysis, for instance whether one is interested in the impact of alternative child benefit systems, or whether a country's legal structure for marriage and divorce are subject to change.

3.6 A starting point for further research

The motivation for the empirical investigation (analyzing intrafamily time allocation decision based on non-cooperative and dynamic bargaining models) to follow is to add to the empirical evidence for competing models.

Because the empirical studies cited in the preceding section were based upon a static threat point variation, changes of which are equally consistent with both the non-cooperative as well as the dynamic bargaining approach, I will first examine the impact of a dynamically determined threat point in Chapter 4. There a model is proposed where female labor supply is derived from a three-period bargaining model and estimated using the spouses' expected future outside options to marriage as an additional set of explanatory variables. In this way the dynamic and interactive nature of marital status and labor supply decisions can be captured, where each decision has long-term consequences. This allows us to differentiate between the static non-cooperative and the sequential non-cooperative model.

Statistical tests of income pooling and Slutsky symmetry (using German data) would encounter severe identification problems due to joint taxation of married couples and the idea of married couples being a profit-sharing community in Germany. Particularly with regard to the tax system, reported net wage incomes of married men and women do not provide appropriate measures of the individual income potentials in most cases. In the empirical studies to follow the focus will therefore be on exogenous determinants of family members' bargaining positions, with special emphasis on the age variables: In

Chapter 5 the relation between spouses' age difference and the division of household work is investigated. With the non-cooperative Bolin model as a starting point, I will present an application of the age-related power argument to the intrafamily division of household work. It will be shown that for German couples the difference between spouses' ages does in fact have an impact on family time allocation, but that the impact is on home time rather than on market time. Chapter 7 is an attempt to quantify the importance of the female "biological clock" for the determination of male/female weights in the bargaining process and hence for individual family members' leisure time. A sharing rule for leisure, that has been derived from a temporarily static non-cooperative bargaining model, is estimated allowing for the influence of the "biological clock" and other bargaining factors.

4 The strategic aspect of female labor supply

4.1 Introduction

Over the past decades there has been an enormous increase in the labor force participation of married women. Whereas overall participation rates in Germany have been falling due to a reduction in life time work (later entry into the labor force as well as earlier retirement), married women's participation rates for age 25 to 50 have almost doubled from the 1960s up to the 1990s, going from 37% to 70% (Franz 1996 and Statistisches Bundesamt 1997). Over this same period divorce rates have continuously increased as well. The probability of divorce in 25 years of marriage has doubled from 15% for a couple that married in 1960 to 30% for a marriage entered in 1980 (Statistisches Bundesamt 1990). Whether the increasing risk of divorce is caused by higher female labor force participation, as many studies suggest, or whether married women now supply more labor due to the higher risk of divorce, as other studies argue (see for instance Diekmann (1991)), the decision to work certainly involves an aspect of insurance that has been missed by traditional models of household labor supply. It is this insurance aspect that will be incorporated in the theoretical modeling and econometric estimation of female labor supply in the present chapter.

In the conventional common preference or unitary model of the household (Becker 1965, Gronau 1973 and 1977) time allocation decisions of family members involve neither human capital considerations of job experience nor strategic bargaining aspects of individual control over financial resources. Instead individual labor supply is derived from the maximization of a household utility function subject to budget and time constraints. Apart from the fact that it still remains to be clarified just how such a joint utility function can be developed, whether it be a social welfare function of the sort proposed by Paul Samuelson (1956), the utility function of an altruistic "head of the household" as Gary Becker suggested (in 1974b) or some other aggregation of the individual utility functions of all family members, the traditional framework fails to fully explain the actual labor force participation of married women. In particular with respect to the opportunity costs of raising children, women are often observed to work for much less than what could possibly be the value of their home time.[21]

Part of the discrepancy between observation and traditional economic theory was taken up by Lehrer and Nerlove (1981). In their human capital framework to model labor supply and fertility behavior of married women, the life cycle is divided into three stages distinguished by the presence and age of children or, interpreted somewhat differently, the demand for household production. A wife allocates her time between work in the labor force, work at home and leisure. She also chooses investment in her own human capital which affects her wage rate in subsequent periods. If the increase in future earnings is sufficiently large, she will work in the labor market even if her wage does not reach the shadow price of her time spent at home rearing children.

Besides the goal of maintaining their human capital and the fear of reducing future chances on the labor market after the child-rearing phase, many women state that they want to achieve some independence from their husbands' earnings[22]. Often this means working for a lower wage rate than predicted by the unitary model. Strategic behavior and its distributional aspect of control over financial resources thus seems to play some role in individual decision making within families. Empirical studies (e.g. the survey by Diekmann and Klein, 1991) indicate that in the light of "fading family stability" and increasing divorce rates, labor force participation also serves as an insurance against the risk of economic losses as a result of divorce.

This strategic aspect of labor force participation was first taken into consideration by economists following a game theoretic approach. In their seminal contributions Marilyn Manser and Murray Brown (1980) as well as Marjorie McElroy and Mary Jean Horney (1981) applied Nash cooperative bargaining theory to household decision making. In these models the distribution of utility within households is determined by the feasible consumption set of the two partners and their outside options[23] which are the single-state utilities. Any change in the relative conflict payoffs, e.g. an increase in income of one of the partners, will affect the household utility distribution towards that spouse's favor.

---

[21] This is true especially in light of the German tax system (Ehegattensplitting), where through joint taxation for married couples the second earner's market work is discouraged since (in most cases) her earnings are hit by high marginal tax rates.

[22] See e.g. Gaugler et al. (1984).

[23] The terms outside option, threat point and conflict payoff are used synonymously. They all indicate a person's best alternative to the bargaining outcome.

An alternative Nash bargaining model with non-cooperative marriage reflecting traditional gender roles instead of divorce as the outside option was proposed by Lundberg and Pollak (1993)[24]. The separate-spheres model, in contrast to the divorce-threat model, also explains different equilibrium distributions in existing marriages implied by transfer payments to either of the partners, even if these do not affect the single state utilities.

Notburga Ott (1992) has taken account of intertemporal dependencies of household decisions through a dynamic bargaining model with subgame consistency. In such a setting the partners' outside options are no longer exogenous, instead they are endogenously determined by the preceding period's time allocation. An individual's decision to supply labor is made allowing for the accompanying impact on her future conflict payoff. The partners' relative bargaining powers therefore directly depend on past time use decisions and the resulting human capital accumulation. Sequential non-cooperation means binding contracts between the periods are not possible. This framework seems to be most appropriate for explaining the labor force participation of many women, who not only regard current labor income but also the human capital dimension of job experience as well as their future bargaining power within the household when making their time allocation decisions.

This chapter is divided into two parts: In the theoretical part a dynamic bargaining model of family time use is presented, in the empirical second part an econometric estimation of female labor supply will incorporate implications of the theoretical model.

In the following section I propose a dynamic bargaining model that extends the work of Ott (1992). Time allocation is determined by intrafamily bargaining taking place within a three-period life cycle. Whereas in the first stage human capital investments are made non-cooperatively by each individual, in subsequent stages, i.e. the family phase, time allocation decisions (esp. housework vs. labor market activity) are determined through Nash bargaining between partners with separation as their threat point. In this model rational individuals not only tend to overinvest in human capital during the first period of life but also have an incentive to choose suboptimal time patterns at the beginning of the family phase should this improve their bargaining position in the following period. This result is due to an asymmetry of the learning effects from market work versus housework and to the asymmetry of the marketability of the different labor skills. Unless binding long-term contracts can be made between the partners, rational behavior always leads to inefficient outcomes with respect to time allocation and household production within the family. In this model labor supply decisions are also determined by

---

[24] Woolley (1988) as well as Konrad/Lommerud (1996) also model intrafamily decision making as a Nash bargaining model with internal threat points.

strategic bargaining considerations, thereby extending the traditional framework.

In the econometric part of the study these strategic aspects are taken into account when estimating female labor supply using data from the German Socio-economic Panel. First the data set is introduced and a comparison of sample characteristics by incidence of future divorce is presented. The apparent interdependence between participation and marital stability suggests that labor supply might in fact be caused by the individual risk of divorce. A three-step estimation procedure is carried out for a model specification that includes "virtual conflict payoffs". A loglinear duration model on marital "survival" or stability is estimated. The resulting conditional probabilities of divorce serve as weights for the conflict payoffs obtained from sub-sample OLS conflict payoff equation estimates. The resulting expected conflict payoffs are then entered into probit estimation of labor force participation. By explicitly including the individual outside option, the resulting labor supply equation allows for strategic aspects of intrafamily time allocation.

The chapter concludes with a summary of the theoretical and empirical results from analyzing labor supply within a dynamic bargaining framework and proposes directions for further research.

4.2 A dynamic bargaining model

I consider a model in which an individual's life cycle is divided into three periods of differing length: In the first period decisions on human capital investment are made, that is, the available time has to be allocated between education activities K and leisure L. [25] At the beginning of the second period each individual is randomly matched to a partner with whom he or she forms a family in order to raise children[26]. The second and the third period constitute the family phase, when time is allocated among three competing activities: work in the labor force M, which yields market goods, work at home H, which yields home produced goods such as child services, and leisure L which yields direct utility. The two periods are distinguished by the children's age or their demand for care (i.e. household production), respectively. This takes a high value in period 2 when infants have to be looked after 24 hours a day and, from a certain age on, diminishes steadily in the late family

[25] This model extends the work of Ott (1992, 1995) by including these pre-family human capital decisions.

[26] In this model the term 'family' generally describes a household in which two persons mutually agree on living together and where a substantial amount of household 'jobs' have to be taken care of. These jobs do not necessarily have to be linked to the bearing and rearing of children, they could also include the nursing of relatives in need of care.

phase.[27] Whereas in the first period time allocation and consumption decisions are made independently by each individual, the family phase is characterized by a two-stage cooperative Nash bargaining game: the distribution of leisure and a composite consumption good within the household is, according to the axiomatic Nash solution of the game, determined by the maximum product of the individual cooperation gains in the two stages. Agreements made at the beginning of the family phase are only binding for one period. Human capital accumulation in one period does not take effect until the subsequent period. Hence, the outside options and the payoff space in the second and third period are determined by decisions made in the prevailing preperiod. Although each individual's utility function is intertemporally separable, the life periods are nonetheless interrelated through the determination of the conflict payoffs. Because of this interdependence the three-stage optimization problem has to be solved through backwards induction according to the idea of subgame consistency.

The optimization problem of spouse a is illustrated with the following overview:

- life cycle:

$$U_1^a + U_2^a + U_3^a \rightarrow \left(U_2^a + U_3^a - C_2^a\right)\left(U_2^b + U_3^b - C_2^b\right) \rightarrow \left(U_3^a - C_3^a\right)\left(U_3^b - C_3^b\right)$$

- time use:

K, L_1	M_2, H_2, L_2	M_3, H_3, L_3

- Backwards induction:

$$U_1^a + W^a \leftarrow \left(U_2^a + V^a - C^a\right)\left(U_2^b + V^b - C^b\right) \leftarrow \left(U_3^a - C_3^a\right)\left(U_3^b - C_3^b\right)$$

Where $U_t^a\left(X_t^a, L_t^a\right)$ and $U_t^b\left(X_t^b, L_t^b\right)$ are individual utility functions depending on the level of private consumption X_t^i and the amount of leisure time L_t^i, with i=a,b. V^a, V^b, W^a and W^b are so-called "maximum-Nash-

[27] The exact age of distinction between stage 2 and stage 3 depends on the institutional circumstances regarding the amount of child care services provided publicly. Whereas U.S.-American studies often differentiate between families with preschool children and those with children of school age, German families with children reaching school age certainly do not enter the third stage as this means even less institutionally provided child care than in kindergarten; here, the distinguishing age level has to be assumed much higher.

solution functions" of the partners a and b at time t. C^a and C^b are the corresponding conflict payoffs. The conflict payoff as the solution to the maximization of single-state utility represents the maximum utility that could be achieved outside the partnership[28]. In other words, it reflects the opportunity costs of family life that are determined by individual productivity factors, such as wage rate w, household productivity z, and non-labor income I: $C^i\left(w^i, z^i, I^i\right)$.

The solution to the three-period model is derived recursively as follows:

Period 3: $\max\left(U_3^a - C_3^a\right)\left(U_3^b - C_3^b\right) \quad \rightarrow V^a, V^b$

Period 2: $\max\left(U_2^a + V^a - C^a\right)\left(U_2^b + V^b - C^b\right) \quad \rightarrow W^a, W^b$

Period 1: $\max \quad U_1^i + W^i \quad \text{for } i = a, b$

First, the conditional bargaining solution for period 3 will yield "maximum-Nash-solution functions" V^a and V^b which depend on time allocation decisions made in the preceding period. Using these indirect utility functions the decision problem of the second period will be solved, again providing "maximum-Nash-solution functions" W^a and W^b for this period. The same procedure is then repeated for the first period.

Period 3

$$\max N_3 = \left(U_3^a\left(X_3^a, L_3^a\right) - C_3^a\right)\left(U_3^b\left(X_3^b, L_3^b\right) - C_3^b\right)$$
$$= \left(U^a - C^a\right)\left(U^b - C^b\right)$$

where $\quad X^a + X^b = X = X_M + X_H \quad$ and $\quad X_H = Z\left(H^a + H^b\right)$

subject to $\quad T = M^i + H^i + L^i \quad \text{for } i = a, b$

and $\quad w^a M^a + w^b M^b - X^a - X^b + Z\left(H^a + H^b\right) + I^a + I^b = 0$

In this last period a static Nash-bargaining game has to be solved. The product of the individual cooperation gains is maximized with regard to private consumption X^i and leisure L^i, subject to budget and time constraints. The private consumption goods of the two partners can either be produced at

---

[28] It is assumed that such important decisions concerning labor force participation and home work justify the use of the divorce-threat model as opposed to fall backs with non-cooperative behavior (see the discussion in the introduction to this chapter or the theoretical survey in Chapter 2).

home (X_H) according to the household production function Z or purchased on the market. The total amount of market goods X_M must not exceed pooled household income generated by labor income $w^aM^a+w^bM^b$ plus non-labor income I^a+I^b [29]

Optimal time allocation in this static setting is known from traditional results, i.e. in equilibrium time is allocated among market work and household production according to the equality between the prevailing productivity factors w^i and z^i (with $z^i = \frac{\partial Z}{\partial H^i}$) and the marginal utility of leisure relative to that of consumption: $\frac{U_L^i}{U_X^i} = z^i = w^i$.

As in the Beckerian framework different wages for men and women lead to specialization of the partners according to their comparative advantages.

The main distinction between this static bargaining model and the traditional model lies in the distribution of utility within the family. Whereas in the common preference theory the question of intrafamily distribution is simply ignored, here it is conditioned on the relative bargaining positions of the partners. Thus, a rise in a's conflict payoff, e.g. due to an increase in this spouse's non-labor income, results in an intrafamily redistribution favoring a.

$$\frac{U_X^a}{U_X^b} = \frac{U^a - C^a}{U^b - C^b}$$

and

$$\frac{U_L^a}{U_L^b} = \frac{w^a}{w^b}\left(\frac{U^a - C^a}{U^b - C^b}\right) = \frac{z^a}{z^b}\left(\frac{U^a - C^a}{U^b - C^b}\right)$$

Period 2

The optimization problem of the second period is solved using the "maximum-Nash-solution functions" $U_{N3}^{a*} = U_3^a\left(X_3^{a*}, L_3^{a*}\right)$ and $U_{N3}^{b*} = U_3^b\left(X_3^{b*}, L_3^{b*}\right)$ from the bargaining game above. With $U_{N3}^{i*} = V^i\left(w_3^a, w_3^b, z_3^a, z_3^b, I_3^a, I_3^b\right)$, V^i is determined by time allocation decisions made in period 2 since wage rates and household productivities depend on learning effects from the prevailing time uses. Second period's time allocation is then optimized according to:

---

29 The price of the market good is set to unity.

$$\max\ N = \left(U_2^a + U_3^a - C^a\right)\left(U_2^b + U_3^b - C^b\right)$$
$$= \left(U^a + V^a - C^a\right)\left(U^b + V^b - C^b\right)$$

subject to budget and time constraints as above.

For the optimal level of M_2^a the following condition must be satisfied:

$$(4.1)\ \frac{U_L^a}{U_X^a} = z^a = w^a + \frac{1}{U_X^a}\left(\frac{\partial V^a}{\partial M_2^a} + \frac{\partial V^a}{\partial C^a}\frac{dC^a}{M_2^a}\right) + \frac{1}{U_X^b}\left(\frac{\partial V^b}{\partial M_2^a} + \frac{\partial V^b}{\partial C^a}\frac{dC^a}{M_2^a}\right)$$

If equality holds, time will be allocated among market work, work at home and leisure according to the marginal outputs of these time uses[30]. In contrast to the traditional framework the marginal output of labor is not confined to the hourly wage rate but also includes the impact of current labor force participation on next period's utility.

If the individual wage rate is positively related to the human capital accumulated, hence a function of the form $w_t = w\left(K, \sum_{t=1}^{t-1} M_t\right)$ with $\frac{\partial w}{\partial K} > 0$, $\frac{\partial^2 w}{\partial^2 K} < 0$, $\frac{\partial w}{\partial M_t} > 0$ and $\frac{\partial^2 w}{\partial^2 M_t} < 0$, the decision to work will have differing long-run effects: Due to a higher wage level an enlargement of the feasible consumption set, that is an outward shift of the utility possibility frontier, will result. I call this the pure frontier effect. At the same time a change of the conflict payoff will lead to a distributional bargaining effect. Both frontier effect and distributional bargaining effect arise from the impact of market work on own and spouse's future utility weighted by the reciprocals of the respective marginal utilities of consumption $\frac{1}{U_X^a}$ and $\frac{1}{U_X^b}$, respectively. Since time spent in the labor market typically has the described positive impact on future utility through a shift of the utility possibility frontier as well as an improved bargaining position, time is allocated to market work even at a wage rate much below household productivity. Hence, in comparison with traditional theory relatively more time will be dedicated to market work and less to household production. Even at $z = w$ a specialization

[30] For simplicity the marginal benefit of household work is restricted to the actual household productivity z while paid labor also yields human capital effects. A consideration of human capital accumulation in household production, however, would not alter the results qualitatively as long as the human capital gained from specialization in the household is less marketable than the human capital accumulated in market work.

in market work takes place. This is due to the asymmetry between the accompanying learning effects resulting from the lower marketability of household abilities. Or, in other words, the differing effects from investments in market-specific human capital and investments in family-specific human capital on bargaining power counter-effect the advantages of specialization.

Considering the long-run effects of time use, i.e. the marginal output of time spent in market production as opposed to time spent in household production, even different wage structures of men and women do not necessarily lead to complete specialization as would be the case in traditional theory. Instead, the interior solution of both partner's time being allocated to all different time uses, to paid as well as unpaid work in particular, that one observes in reality can now be explained.

Labor supply in the early family phase can be described as a function of both spouses' wages, household productivities, nonlabor incomes and outside options to family life:

$$M_2^i = M^i\left(w^a, w^b, z^a, z^b, I^a, I^b, C^a, C^b\right) \qquad \text{for } i=a,b.$$

Period 1

The optimization problem of the first period is solved using the "maximum-Nash-solution functions" $U_{N2}^{a*} = U_{a2}\left(X_2^{a*}, L_2^{a*}\right)$ and $U_{N2}^{b*} = U_{b2}\left(X_2^{b*}, L_2^{b*}\right)$ from the bargaining game above. With $U_{N2}^{i*} = W^i\left(w_2^a, w_2^b, z_2^a, z_3^b, I_2^a, I_2^b\right)$, W^i is determined by time allocation decisions made in period 1. Although partners have not met yet, they know that their expected utility will also be determined by their future partner's human capital investments in the first period where all potential matching partners are simply assumed to be equal. Now, first period's time use is optimized according to:

$$\max U_1^i + U_2^i + U_3^i$$
$$= U^i + W^i$$

subject to $$T = M^i + K^i + L^i$$

and $$w^i M^i + I^i - X^i \geq 0 \quad \text{for } i = a, b$$

Since in the pre-family stage decisions on time use are made independently, individual maximization is now subject to individual budget constraints.

Optimal time allocation decisions have to meet the first order condition:

(4.2)
$$\frac{U_L^i}{U_X^i} = \frac{1}{U_X^i}\left(\frac{\partial W^i}{\partial K^i} + \frac{\partial W^i}{\partial C^i}\frac{dC^i}{dK^i}\right)$$

The amount of educational investment should be chosen so as to equalize the shadow price of time and the marginal benefit associated with an additional unit of schooling. Since human capital investment takes effect on future wage rates, the marginal output of education has two components: The first is the direct impact of education on utility possibilities, the frontier effect, the second is the distributional bargaining effect that arises from a change of the individual conflict payoff. More human capital leads to higher returns from market work and thus improves the financial situation of the household as a whole. At the same time it strengthens the individual bargaining power through an improvement of the single state utility.

Due to these long-run effects of time use more human capital investment will typically result in comparison with traditional theory or even compared with the dynamic model of Lehrer/Nerlove which explicitly considers human capital accumulation.

4.2.1 Implications

Since in the family phase the distribution of utility within the household is uniquely determined by the utility possibility frontier of the two partners as well as their outside options, all decisions that affect these parameters are of great importance for the intrafamily allocation of time. The amount of human capital investment chosen by each individual in the first period of life will set the base for the family bargaining game in the following periods with regard to the origin of the feasible payoff space and the conflict payoff. Likewise, intrafamily time allocation in the second period has implications not only for that period's outcome but decisively determines the partner's bargaining positions in the next family phase (3rd period).

Pre-family human capital investment

There are two effects resulting from any change in human capital investment: a shift of the utility possibility frontier and an altered division of resources between the partners. Starting from a given optimal education level, i.e. for efficient choices in the pre-family stage, the frontier effect of an extra unit of schooling (see equation (4.2)) has to be zero. The distributional bargaining effect, however, induces a move along the efficiency frontier favoring a so that a has an incentive to overinvest in human capital compared to the household-efficient level K^{a*}. Overinvestment occurs as long as

$$\frac{dC^a}{dK^a} > \frac{\partial U^a}{\partial L^a} \tag{4.3}$$

that is, as long as, by accumulating an extra unit of human capital exceeding the efficient level, the improvement of a's bargaining position is higher than her utility loss from reduced leisure time in period 1. This condition holds if optimal human capital investment as single is higher than within a family[31].

In traditional models no incentive for overinvestment exists. Since the outside option is neglected, the total effect of an extra unit of education would be zero[32]. The traditional result could therefore be considered as a special case of the bargaining approach where optimal human capital investment as single equals that within a family. Hence, education exceeding the optimal level would have no effect on the individual bargaining position.

As opposed to the human capital model by Lehrer and Nerlove (1981) where the optimal level of investment in human capital is a function of the extent to which this capital is utilized in the subsequent stages of life, here the human capital endowment serves for improving the individual bargaining position regardless of its actual utilization. In other words, the human capital endowment is employed rather implicitly than explicitly in the time allocation decision. It serves as a strategic variable in the family decision-making process.

Intrafamily labor supply

Rational individuals not only tend to overinvest in human capital at the pre-family stage but also have an incentive to choose suboptimal time patterns at the beginning of the family phase if this will improve their bargaining position in the following period[33]. Again, there are two effects arising from a change in second period's labor supply on the bargaining set of the late family phase: a shift of the utility possibility frontier and an altered division of

---

[31] This implication corresponds with the results of Konrad and Lommerud's two-stage game of marriage (1996) where the wage rate is chosen non-cooperatively in the first stage and a Nash bargaining game between the partners is solved in the second stage.

[32] A question that also deserved empirical investigation would be: If, as it is not modeled here, investments in human capital also occur because children benefit from a higher educational level of their parents, do mothers and fathers invest differently in that kind of human capital that can be transmitted to children, such as e.g. humanities versus technical skills?

[33] This suboptimal time allocation in the early family phase or the underprovision of household production is comparable to the hold-up problem in industrial economics (see Grossman/Hart 1986 and Hart/Moore 1990). There firms hesitate to make relationship-specific investments due to the threat of expropriation.

resources between the spouses. Since for efficient choices the frontier effect equals zero, an additional unit spent in the labor force does not change the utility space but induces a move on the efficiency frontier towards a higher utility level for a. As we can see from equation (4.1) an oversupply of market work in the second period will occur if, starting from given optimal time allocation, an increase of one partner's labor force participation will raise his or her next-period's conflict payoff (4.4) and if the distributional bargaining effect favoring his or her own future utility exceeds that of the spouse (4.5):

$$\frac{\partial C_2^a}{\partial M_2^a} > 0 \tag{4.4}$$

$$\left| \frac{1}{\partial U_X^a} \frac{\partial V^a}{\partial C_3^a} \right| > \left| \frac{1}{\partial U_X^b} \frac{\partial V^b}{\partial C_3^a} \right| \tag{4.5}$$

The first condition holds if optimal labor supply as single is higher than within a family. In the traditional framework no incentive for oversupply exists. Since the outside option is neglected, the total effect of an extra unit of market work would be zero. The traditional result could therefore be considered as a special case of the bargaining approach where optimal time allocation as single equals that within a family. Hence, labor supply exceeding the optimal level would have no effect on the individual bargaining position. This would also be the case for a setting with binding long-term contracts between the partners, where the individual bargaining powers are assumed to remain unchanged regardless of the chosen time allocation in period 2. Thus the lack of distributional incentives would sustain an optimal level of labor supply. Unless binding long-term contracts can be made between the partners bargaining outcomes will be suboptimal with respect to time allocation and household production[34].

Due to intrafamily bargaining, individual optimization is not exclusively focussed on the maximization of family outcome but also on one's own share of that outcome. Since utility within a household is distributed according to the partner's external alternatives, time allocation decisions have to be made in the light of their effects on these external alternatives. Even though with the presence of small children in the early family phase more time devoted to household production, particularly a specialization of the partners, would be

[34] On a discussion concerning the enforcement of intrafamily agreements see Ott (1993). Another way of dealing with the weakening voice enforcement of marital contracts has been proposed by Kjell Erik Lommerud (1989). He models the relationship between divorce and allocation of time by introducing a probability of divorce that influences a couple's time use in the preceding period.

efficient in the short run, none of the partners will be willing to weaken his or her future bargaining position. As a result, not all production possibilities in the household can be exhausted. On account of educational overinvestment before and suboptimal time allocation within the early family phase the gains from specialization within the household will be less than those technically feasible. In the dynamic bargaining model with endogenously determined conflict payoffs paid labor serves as a strategic variable for intrafamily utility distribution.

4.2.2 Discussion of the theoretical results

In the model presented rational individuals tend to overinvest in human capital in the pre-family period. At the beginning of the family phase they also have an incentive to choose an amount of labor supply exceeding the optimal level or an amount of household production falling short of the optimal level, respectively, should this improve their bargaining position in the following period. Unless binding long-term contracts can be made between the partners, rational behavior always leads to inefficient outcomes with respect to time allocation and household production within the family.

One major implication of intrafamily bargaining concerns the estimation of labor supply. For the reasons just described, the decision to participate in the labor market in the dynamic bargaining approach is not only determined by productivity indicators, such as wage rates and household productivities, but also includes human capital accumulation as well as strategic aspects regarding the individual bargaining position. Allowing for strategic aspects in econometric specification will therefore lead to more satisfactory estimates of individual labor supply.

With its assumption about the time structure of life, this model admittedly describes an extreme case of family formation. Human capital investments are made before partners in life randomly meet and begin to raise families. Another extreme case of lifestyle would be the single state. Reality must lie somewhere in between these two cases. If a probability is assigned to each extreme, then an individual's expected lifetime utility takes some value weighted by the likeliness of these two lifestyles. As for the investment in education, if the probability of staying single is greater than zero and if the sufficient conditions for overinvestment hold, i.e. optimal human capital investments as single are higher than within marriage, even greater overinvestment will result. This is because no one can be sure that he or she will meet "Ms. or Mr. Right" and be able to take advantage from a cooperation surplus, especially that share generated by intrahousehold specialization. Thus, the finding of inefficient educational decisions remains, even in a more general version of the model.

4.3 Empirical implementation of the bargaining effect of labor supply

In this section the strategic aspect of family time use decisions is implemented to estimate female labor supply, taking into account marital stability and the outside option to marriage as determinants of female labor force participation[35]. The empirical implementation is thus focused on the impact of bargaining positions on time allocation in the early family phase taking human capital investments prior to family formation as given.

A number of studies investigated how divorce probabilities influence female labor supply decisions[36]. William R. Johnson and Jonathan Skinner (1986) accounted for the effect of marital stability on labor force participation in estimating a simultaneous model of future divorce probability and current labor supply for married women. Using 1972 data from the Panel Study of Income Dynamics (PSID) for couples who were married in that year and some of whom separated in the following 6 years, Johnson/Skinner's results support the hypothesis that subjective divorce probabilities increase labor supply. In a cross-national comparison Barbara Butrica (1998) finds large differences between the United States and Germany. Her estimates, based on the 1986 samples of the PSID and the German Socio-Economic Panel (GSOEP), suggest that the probability of divorce has no significant impact on labor supply or hours decisions of women in the U.S. whereas Germany very much resembles the Johnson-Skinner results from the U.S. in the 1970s. Kristian Bolin (1996) adopted a similar approach with Swedish data. He also included the risk of divorce as an additional regressor in his labor supply equation. Whereas Johnson/Skinner and Butrica estimated labor supply within marriage, Bolin was interested in labor supply at the time of marriage. His results also convey a significant impact of predicted divorce risks on female labor force participation.

Using 1979 U.S.-data the articles by H. Elizabeth Peters (1986) and Allen M. Parkman (1992) both conclude that the introduction of unilateral divorce has increased the labor force participation rate of married women. But whereas Peters attributes this response to the lack of compensation for marriage-specific investment at divorce that creates an incentive for married women to increase their marketable capital, Parkman brings up the lack of compensa-

---

[35] Theoretically, male labor supply is subject to these strategic considerations just as well. Practically, however, men's working hours show much less variation than women's. Since the model proposed has in any case initially been chosen to motivate the observation of married mothers' labor force participation, the empirical analysis will be restricted to women only.

[36] See Bolin 1997, Butrica 1998, Gray 1998, Haurin 1989, Johnson and Skinner 1986, Parkman 1992, Peters 1986.

tion for married women's reduced human capital. He finds a greater effect of unilateral divorce on the labor supply of younger and better educated women who would experience larger reductions in their future earning capacity should they reduce their participation in the labor force. Although Parkman implicitly considers the dynamic effects of human capital loss for married women, overall the cited studies restrict their analysis to the relationship between labor supply and the risk of divorce as such rather than the impact of the external alternative or outside option to family decision making, i.e. the impact of the underlying bargaining power.

Jeffrey S. Gray (1998) accounts for the relevance of the wife's bargaining position when investigating U.S. married women's labor supply behavior with a change in marital property laws. A state's adoption of unilateral divorce can be interpreted as an exogenous and unexpected shift of the extra-household environmental parameters (EEPs) of family life. In contrast to Peters and Parkman he finds that unilateral divorce as opposed to mutual-consent divorce has no impact on married women's labor force participation unless the underlying marital-property laws in each state are also considered (1998: 629). By analyzing exogenous changes of EEPs, Gray concludes that the wife's labor supply is an increasing function of her bargaining position within marriage.

In this study the empirical application of bargaining power in family decision making is further developed: Women's expected outside options are estimated and their impact on female labor supply are investigated to directly test the theoretical relationship derived in the dynamic bargaining model above, using the concept of a "virtual conflict payoff".

4.3.1 The virtual conflict payoff

The concept of the "virtual conflict payoff" accounts for the endogeneity of individual bargaining power with regard to time use decisions, particularly labor force participation. It is due to the fact that everybody has some outside option to family bargaining regardless of whether it will ever be realized or not. Whereas for separating couples we are able to observe their economic performance after a break-up and, thus, a realization of their outside options to family life, for intact partnerships we do not observe anything about the spouses' conflict payoffs. The basic idea here is to apply whatever can be observed for separating spouses to the non-separating ones in order to generate what may be called a "virtual conflict payoff" for each person no matter whether a household dissolution will actually take place or not. The impact of the virtual or expected conflict payoff on individual time allocation can then be examined. In other words, the strategic aspect to female employment that has been derived in the theoretical model can be investigated empirically. Allowing for human capital and other individual endowment factors, the individual outside option is chosen as an additional determinant of the supply of labor. In this way we extend the conventional estimation of female labor supply by a strategic element[37].

4.3.2 Data set and sample characteristics

To explore the relationship between female labor supply and marital stability in Germany I draw on data from the German Socio-Economic Panel (GSOEP) again. As an individual household micro-data panel the GSOEP is a rich data source for analyzing labor force participation by means of various individual as well as household characteristics. The empirical results to be presented here are based on data from the West German sub-sample of the GSOEP covering the years from 1985 to 1997. Making use of the panel structure of the data, the long-term impact of the risk of divorce on current labor supply is accounted for: a cross-section sample of couples that have been married in 1985 (2nd wave of the GSOEP) is analyzed having additional information on their marital status as well as their economic status in the twelve subsequent years until 1997. To maximize the number of observations we use an unbalanced panel, taking account of data censoring. The analysis is restricted to German couples with the wife not younger than 20 and not older than 45 years of age (to roughly cover the early-family-phase age) and the husband between 20 and 55 years (to prevent the results from being excessively affected by retirement behavior). It is further restricted to couples where both spouses have completed their schooling or apprenticeship in 1985, in order to confine the analysis to time allocation decisions made in the second period when (according to the theoretical model) human capital investments in education have already been completed. As we are interested in the labor force participation of dependent employees only, all self-employed are dropped as well as all those working in the farming sector. Observations with missing data on any of the explaining variables have also been removed. The final sample consists of 751 couples, 94 of whom separated or divorced in one of the subsequent years[38], 432 of whom remained married during the following

---

[37] The simultaneous modeling of time allocation decisions and household dissolution characterizes an extension of the conventional estimation procedures for female labor supply (for an overview of the empirical literature see e.g. Layard et al. 1980, Killingsworth 1983, Killingsworth/Heckman 1986, Mroz 1987 and Blundell/MaCurdy 1998).

[38] The sample is not limited to "complete" couples, though. In other words it partly consists of women whose husbands have left the panel at some stage and it includes men whose wives did not participate in the interviews during the whole time period. To be precise, information on 432 women living in stable marriages and 94 separating women is used together with the observations of 427 non-separating and 86 separating men.

12-year period (balanced panel) and 225 of whom dropped out of the sample eventually (unbalanced panel).

Table 4.1: Sample characteristics in 1985

	Non-separating Sample		Separating Sample	
	Mean	(Standard deviation)	Mean	(Standard deviation)
Age wife	33.28	(6.42)	30.69	(6.63)
Age husband	35.90	(5.96)	33.57	(6.92)
Years of schooling wife	10.96	(1.81)	10.96	(1.96)
Years of schooling husband	11.77	(2.51)	11.08	(2.14)
Current labor force participation wife (%)	0.44	(0.50)	0.49	(0.50)
Current labor force participation husband (%)	0.88	(0.32)	0.83	(0.38)
Hours of work wife	13.30	(16.66)	15.87	(17.03)
Hours of work husband	38.04	(9.00)	36.55	(12.13)
Work experience while married, wife (%)	0.56	(0,37)	0.61	(0.38)
Work experience while married, husband (%)	0.88	(0,22)	0.89	(0.22)
Dummy First marriage	0.92	(0.27)	0.89	(0.31)
Years married	10.74	(6.27)	8.66	(6.23)
Age at marriage wife	22.51	(3.90)	22.03	(4.38)
Age at marriage husband	25.13	(3.98)	24.91	(4.62)
Dummy Child < 16 years	0.77	(0.42)	0.79	(0.41)
Age of youngest child (<16 years)	6.58	(5.01)	5.45	(4.51)
n	432		94	

Data source: German Socio-Economic Panel 1985-1997.

In Table 4.1 the summary statistics of the two sub-samples, based on women with high marital stability versus separating women, are listed. The two groups reveal great differences in their human capital endowment, their current labor force participation and in personal characteristics regarding marital background variables. The average non-separating couple is older than a separating couple[39] and it got married at a slightly older age. Also the share of first marriages is substantially higher with stable partnerships.

Non-separating women are on average less educated (i.e. less years of schooling), have less work experience in full-time and part-time employment during marriage and their current labor force participation and monthly work hours are lower than those of divorcing women. Their husbands, on the contrary, have more work experience and are currently working to a higher extent than their separating counterparts. The presence and the age of children do not make a big difference as we are comparing couples' characteristics at year 1985 when separation might still be a number of years ahead.

Overall we can say that differences with regard to human capital endowment and labor force status are smaller among separating spouses. Female and male education, work experiences, current labor force participation and hours of work are generally more equated in the separating subgroup. These complementarities within "stable" couples might be an indication for the Beckerian argument of comparative advantages. That is, with diminishing gender differences the returns from specialization within the household are losing importance. For the separating sub-sample the gains from staying married will turn out to be lower on average.

As a first finding we may note that the descriptive statistics provide a weak support of the insurance aspect to female employment derived above.

4.3.3 Female labor force participation with virtual conflict payoffs

The labor supply function to be estimated is specified according to the following equation:

$$M_i = X_i'\beta + C_i^{*}{}'\gamma + \varepsilon_i \quad i = 1,..,N$$

where X_i is a vector of variables commonly used as regressors in an estimation of labor supply (consisting of education, age, previous work experience, children, household nonlabor income and husband's earnings). According to the model the bargaining position is included as a vector C_i^* containing a set of (latent) bargaining variables. The effects of omitted variables are represented by the random error term ε_i.

---

[39] Of course, this pattern is a rather mechanical one: In a given population the average age of a couple to be separated is always lower than the overall age mean of couples, since the proportion of unstable marriages decreases over time.

4.3.4 Bargaining variables

In the theoretical model presented above family partners bargain over the distribution of utility according to their relative bargaining positions. But how is this bargaining power determined empirically, in every day life so to speak? Presumably there is nobody explicitly computing his or her conflict payoff to be realized in the case of a divorce. In a more subtle way, however, every person becomes aware of conflict payoff measures when observing friends, relatives or neighbors who separate. One might argue that each individual applies such a bargaining measure to his or her own situation, given individual human capital endowment, household characteristics and extra-household environmental parameters (EEP). In other words, it is the perceived bargaining power drawn from personal observations and expectations that we suspect to affect intrafamily decision making. Next those bargaining variables will be introduced that are assumed to characterize the perceived bargaining power and used as explanatory variables in the final labor supply estimation.

The probability of divorce

Since the empirical studies cited above and the descriptive statistics above suggest that a wife's probability of divorce is related to her labor supply decision, we will include the individual probability of divorce in the estimation of female labor force participation. A duration model for marital stability will be estimated to provide individual hazards for divorce conditional on the tenure of marriage. The cumulative divorce probability for the subsequent ten-year period will be used as one of the explaining variables representing perceived bargaining power in the labor supply equation.

The conflict payoff measure

In order to consider the individual outside option in the labor supply equation, expected conflict payoffs have to be generated for those spouses who do not separate within the sample period and hence do not yield any information on their fall back position explicitly. Consider a payoff equation for the latent conflict payoff c_i^* of the form

$$c_i^* = \tau \cdot Z_i + u_i \quad i = 1,\dots,N$$

where Z_i is a vector of variables observed for all divorced men and women, including the tenure of marriage, human capital and other socio-demographic and household variables, and u_i is a mean zero normally distributed random error term representing the effects of unobserved factors. Since c_i^* is only known for the separating subgroup (d=1), one observes:

$$c_i = c_i^* \quad \text{if } d = 1$$

$$c_i = 0 \quad \text{if } d = 0$$

The conflict payoff actually drawn from the separating group is computed as the monthly adjusted equivalent income in the second year after break-up according to $inc_e = hhinc/(hhsize)^{0.5}$. Hence, household income is divided by the square root of the number of household members to roughly allow for economies of scale in household consumption. Since during the twelve months following a separation entitlements to transfer payments have in most cases not been settled yet, reported incomes turn out to be subject to heavy variation. Therefore I decided to use the second year's financial status (after separation) as a more robust measure of a spouse's conflict payoff[40].

Since the group of separated respondents might differ from the group of still married spouses on account of unobserved variables, the problem of sample selection bias should be carefully considered when assigning conflict payoffs to non-separating wives and husbands. Otherwise the use of predicted conflict payoffs obtained from an Ordinary Least Squares (OLS) estimation based on separating respondents only, might result in inconsistent parameter estimates due to sample selectivity problems. Therefore, the Heckman procedure for selectivity bias-corrected estimations (Heckman 1979, 1980) should be applied to the estimation of consistent conflict payoffs. When applying the two-stage Heckman procedure to the estimation of conflict payoffs, however, no robust estimation results could be obtained due to collinearity problems and the very small sample size of separating couples (n=94 or 86, respectively). As simulation studies show (Puhani 1997, Rendtel 1992), in those cases sub-sample OLS still turns out to be the most robust estimator. As a consequence, we estimate conflict payoffs using the sub-sample of separating couples. Once the payoff estimation coefficients have been obtained, virtual conflict payoffs can be predicted for the whole sample and for every subsequent year, based on the respondents' socio-demographic characteristics. This virtual conflict payoff, averaged over the ten-year period with the weights according to the conditional divorce probabilities, is then used within the set of explaining variables for perceived bargaining power in the labor supply equation.

40 It could be argued that a woman's individual income rather than her share of the household income represents her conflict payoff in case of a divorce. On the other hand, the measure used should account for the possibility of a new partnership and the accommodating financial resources that are part of the EEPs.

Relative bargaining power

Relative bargaining power within the household as a determinant of the strategic supply of labor can enter the estimation equation in various ways. In the theoretical model it is the relative bargaining coefficient, reflected by one partner's gain from bargaining divided by that of the other spouse, which conditions the individual time use decision. In the empirical analysis I therefore also use a relative measure of individual bargaining power, namely the ratio of the wife's and the husband's average predicted conflict payoffs to capture strategic behavior within the household.

This way the wife's bargaining position enters her labor force participation equation in a two-folded manner, with an absolute term reflecting the *absolute level* of her bargaining position and with a relative term reflecting her *comparative* bargaining position within the household.

4.3.5 Estimation procedure

The resulting three-step estimation procedure is performed as displayed in Figure 4.1: In the first step a loglinear duration model (Weibull model) on marital "survival" or stability is estimated for the full unbalanced sample of all married couples.

Figure 4.1: Three-step estimation procedure

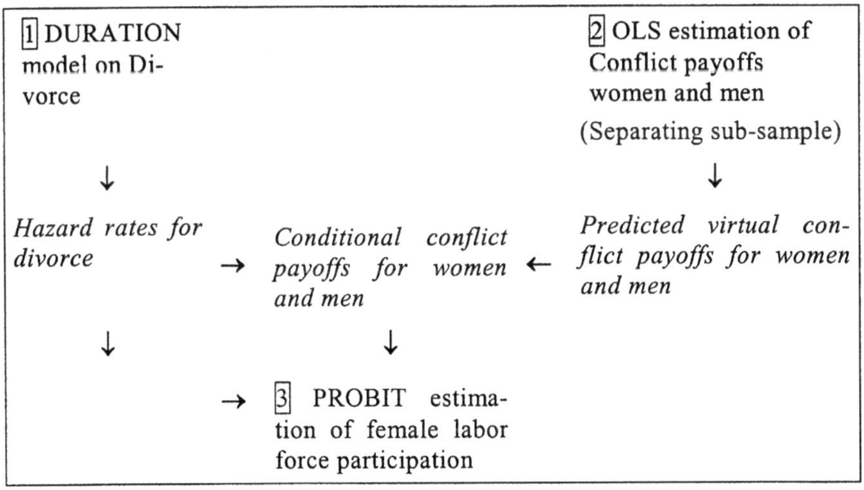

The effect of a set of exogenous variables y_i on the hazard function can be formalized by writing (Diekmann/Mitter 1984, Greene 1993):

$$r(t) = \lambda p \cdot (\lambda t)^{p-1}$$

with $$\lambda = e^{-\beta' y_i}.$$

The resulting hazard rates yield probabilities of divorce conditional on the tenure of the marriage. Hence, divorce probabilities can be predicted for each spouse for each year of his or her (average) remaining lifetime.

In the second step male and female OLS conflict payoff equations are estimated using the separating sub-sample only. Average expected conflict payoffs are then computed for all men and women weighted by the hazards of divorce. Together with the cumulative individual probability of a separation within the next ten-year period these conditional conflict payoffs are in the third step entered as imputed variables into the Probit estimation of labor force participation.

4.3.6 Empirical findings

The estimation of the loglinear duration model reveals that marital stability is significantly higher the greater the difference in husband's and wife's educational backgrounds (Table 4.2). It is also higher for first marriages. The level of schooling and the spouses' age difference, in comparison, are not statistically significantly related to separation in this model.

Table 4.2: Step 1 - Duration model for marital stability

WEIBULL (nw=1065)	Duration of marriage	
	Coeff. est.	Stand. dev.
Years of schooling wife	-0.003	0.569
Difference in years of schooling husband-wife	0.125	0.040
Age at marriage wife	0.019	0.019
Difference in age at marriage husband-wife	0.023	0.018
First marriage - dummy	0.715	0.263
σ	0.660	0.073
Constant	3.322	0.564
- Log Likelihood	418	

Data source: German Socio-Economic Panel 1985-1997.

The coefficient estimate for $\sigma = 1/p < 1$ indicates that the hazard function of divorce is monotonically increasing with the years of marriage[41]. Since $p \neq 1$, the Weibull model does not collapse to the exponential model with a constant hazard rate. Given the estimated coefficients we can now compute conditional probabilities for each individual to have a divorce in any of the subsequent years and derive a cumulative divorce probability for the following ten-year period.

The second-step coefficient estimates for the conflict payoff equation are listed in Table 4.3. For illustrative purposes, the results presented here are based on a more extensive specification of the conflict payoff. The predicted values for the full sample will be derived from a subset of these explanatory variables to reduce multi-collinearity problems in the preceding steps.

Here the conflict payoff measure has been regressed on human capital variables and household characteristics. Equations for women and men have been estimated separately to take account of gender differences. Indeed, the conflict payoff determination of women and men turns out to differ substantially as can be seen with the coefficient estimates. Whereas the outside option for married men is positively related to their own work experience at the year preceding separation and inversely related to the years already married, women's conflict payoffs are higher if their partners have worked part-time, with a better household's financial status and if they are re-married to a new partner after divorce.

Separating couples might still differ from non-separating in a systematic way that is not independent of conflict payoffs. As mentioned above, data constraints prevent us from using the Heckman procedure to correct for a potential selection bias. The last variable, indicating whether the divorcee is living with a new partner, has been included to capture at least part of this selection rule that cannot be explained by the human capital variables used.

In order to compute the expected conflict payoff, those characteristics that are strictly monotonically increasing over time, such as age and the tenure of marriage, are appropriately adjusted, whereas variables such as total household income and number of household members are set constant (static expectations). Work experience is also reassessed according to the present (i.e. 1985) labor force status. The final conflict payoff measure is then computed as the weighted average of expected future conflict payoffs, with the weights according to individual divorce probabilities in all years. To predict conflict

[41] To illustrate, an average couple faces a conditional probability to have a divorce in the next year (i.e. 1986) of 0.1%, the conditional probability for a divorce in the tenth year (1995) is 1%, for the 30st year it is 1.7%.

payoffs for the non-separating sample a subset specification is used to minimize multi-collinearity problems later on[42].

Table 4.3: Step 2 - OLS estimation of the conflict payoff

OLS (n_w=94/ n_h=86)	Conflict payoff			
	Wife		Husband	
	Coeff. est.	Stand. dev.	Coeff. est.	Stand. dev.
Age	-7.67	16.99	-32.17	31.94
Education	51.39	39.64	118.19	66.42
Work experience full-time	-4.08	17.54	64.88	33.65
Work experience part-time	-10.35	19.62	652.85	172.87
Work experience full-time, partner	13.33	39.21	49.21	28.84
Work experience part-time, partner	242.24	77.66	-4.62	31.77
Total household income	161.67	56.05	171.13	103.20
# of household members	-125.40	70.48	-31.68	112.84
Years married	11.32	41.18	-3.82	1.29
New partner after separation	650.47	179.47	-176.75	385.04
Constant	708.60	608.89	672.97	1007.4
Adjusted R^2	0.24		0.33	

Data source: German Socio-Economic Panel 1985-1997.
Note: The conflict payoff is computed as monthly equivalent income in the second year after separation.

42 For the final conflict payoff equation (for men) age, years of schooling, years in fulltime employment, wife's work experience in fulltime and part-time and the number of household members are included as explanatory variables (R^2=0.36). For women age, years of schooling, husband's work experience in part-time, total household income, the number of household members and a dummy for a new marriage partner are used (R^2=0.27).

Table 4.4: Step 3 - Female labor force participation

PROBIT (n_w=751)	Labor force participation – marginal effects			
	Model I	Model II	Model III	Model IV
Constant	-0.1143 (0.1923)	-0.1090 (0.1923)	-0.2001 (0.1971)	0.2814 (0.2256)
Human capital variables				
Years of schooling	0.0420 (0.0119)	0.0364 (0.0124)	0.0208 (0.01305)	0.0086 (0.0135)
Job experience (hypothetical)	0.0406 (0.0165)	0.0397 (0.0165)	0.03311 (0.0168)	0.0165 (0.0173)
Job experience squared (hyp.)	-0.0012 (0.0005)	-0.0013 (0.0005)	-0.0011 (0.0005)	-0.0009 (0.0005)
Household characteristics				
HH nonlabor income/1000	-0.0483 (0.0314)	-0.0429 (0.0315)	-0.0347 (0.0313)	-0.0669 (0.0323)
Husband's labor income/1000	-0.1045 (0.0232)	-0.0951 (0.0239)	-0.1735 (0.0302)	-0.1494 (0.0304)
Dummy child<16 years	-0.3093 (0.0724)	-0.3178 (0.0726)	-0.3006 (0.0735)	-0.2678 (0.0746)
# children <6 years	-0.2308 (0.0410)	-0.2280 (0.0411)	-0.1713 (0.0427)	-0.2052 (0.0437)
# children 6-16 years	-0.0648 (0.0351)	-0.0684 (0.0353)	-0.0364 (0.0364)	-0.0372 (0.0364)
Bargaining variables				
Probability of divorce		0.5954 (0.3585)	0.6015 (0.3617)	0.9004 (0.3715)
Conflict payoff /1000			0.3145 (0.0679)	0.4760 (0.0762)
Relative bargaining power				-0.8788 (0.1939)
- Log Likelihood	423.24	421.89	411.12	400.52

Data source: German Socio-Economic Panel 1985-1997.
Note: Standard errors in parentheses.[43]

[43] Due to the introduction of imputed variables the standard errors of the probit-estimates have to be interpreted very carefully. Therefore I will not refer to the T-statistics since they might not provide reliable values in order to reject the H_0-hypotheses accurately.

The nested Probit estimation of female labor force participation in the third step (see Table 4.4) reveals that the decision to work is significantly positively related to the probability of divorce as well as to the absolute size of the wife's expected conflict payoff and it is inversely related to her relative bargaining power even when controlling for variables indicating her own and her husband's human capital endowment, the opportunity costs of market work (measured by the presence and age of children) and household non-labor income.

Introducing the cumulative probability of having a divorce within the next ten years in Model II, leaves the coefficient estimates of the standard participation model (Model I) substantively unchanged. The divorce probability alone, however, has hardly any effect on female employment. If one accepts a standard error that amounts to 0.6 of the coefficient estimate, the likeliness of a separation is positively related with women's decision to take up gainful employment. Economically speaking women with unstable marriages are more likely to be working (out of insurance considerations) than women who are living in stable relationships. If the probability of divorce is raised by ten percentage points, labor force participation will increase by 6%.

When in addition the wife's expected conflict payoff, averaged over a period of ten years, is included (Model III), we see that, while the coefficient for divorce probability remains unchanged, female employment becomes more likely the greater the size of the outside option to marriage. A 100-German-Marks rise of the conflict payoff is associated with a 3% higher probability to supply labor to the market. Interpreting this result in accordance with the dynamic model would imply that married women supply labor in order to enhance their future conflict payoff as well as their bargaining power within the household.

As can be seen from the sizes of the standard errors, one might suspect the presence of multi-collinearity between the conflict payoff measure and education as well as one of the children variables, though. The estimates for the variable counting the number of children aged 6-16 in the household suggest that, where children have a negative impact on mothers' employment, strategic considerations lead to an ever higher participation probability of these women.

Including all bargaining variables as explanatory variables in the last model reveals the great impact of a woman's perceived bargaining power on her labor force participation decision. The relation between participation and the ratio of wife's and husband's conflict payoffs is a statistically negative one, i.e. women with weak bargaining positions in comparison to their partners seek to keep their human capital (or bargaining power) from depreciating. Labor force participation gives them the opportunity to reach a certain level of conflict payoff and thereby insures against the risk of divorce or the risk of a renegotiation of utility distribution in the late family phase.[44]

In summary, these results indicate that female labor supply can be, at least partly, led back to strategic considerations regarding the individual future bargaining position. The more unequal a couples' (future) bargaining powers the higher is the wife's incentive to improve her relative bargaining position by staying in the labor market. That is, a woman's relative bargaining position, i.e. the expected relative attractiveness of her own external alternative with respect to that of her partner, significantly determines her employment decision. As predicted by the dynamic bargaining model, the impact of the conflict payoff results in higher labor force participation due to a lower reservation wage level. The insurance aspect is most important for women with poor bargaining positions.

4.4 Conclusions

In the theoretical model presented, rational individuals would be expected to overinvest in human capital in the pre-family period. At the beginning of the family phase they have an incentive to choose an amount of labor supply exceeding the optimal level or an amount of household production falling short of the optimal level, respectively, should this improve their bargaining position in the following period. Unless binding long-term contracts can be made between the partners, rational behavior always leads to inefficient outcomes with respect to time allocation and household production within the family. By taking into account the dynamic implications of different time uses, it turns out that market labor can also be supplied out of strategic reasons. It serves as an insurance against the loss of bargaining power or the risk of divorce.

The empirical results confirm the hypotheses derived for the early family phase: according to the theoretical model, a woman's relative bargaining power, measured as the ratio of her own and her husband's virtual conflict payoffs, is negatively related and the size of her conflict payoff as well as her individual probability of divorce are positively related to her labor force participation. It seems that by staying in the labor market married women intend to keep their human capital and, thus, their bargaining power from depreciating. Labor force participation gives them the opportunity to reach a certain level of conflict payoff. Thus the estimation of labor supply with fitted con-

[44] The schooling variable, however, seems to reflect an endogeneity problem and so does job experience in Model IV: the interdependencies between the human capital variables and an endogenously determined conflict payoff might therefore result in biased coefficient estimates.

flict payoffs derived from payoff equation estimates supports the bargaining argument of a strategic aspect to female employment. As Gray (1998) stated for the U.S., I come to the conclusion that wives' labor supply is an increasing function of their (expected) bargaining position within marriage, if measured in absolute terms. The relative bargaining position has an inverse effect on labor supply, meaning that women with weak bargaining power are more likely to enter employment (as an insurance) even when controlling for other household income.

It could be argued that what I interpreted as strategic behavior within the household might in fact simply be strategic behavior versus the labor market, that women seek to maintain a certain level of human capital regardless of any "strategy" versus their partners. Indeed, the positive relation between female labor supply and the absolute conflict measure does not allow us to distinguish a wife's insurance against divorce from an insurance against human capital depreciation in general. The ratio of conflict payoffs, however, solely reflects a wife's bargaining position relative to that of her husband and thus unambiguously provides an indication of strategic behavior *within* the household.

It might further be argued that in face of the German legal structures for marriage and divorce and the primary earner's obligation to pay maintenance to the former spouse after a separation, women do not need an additional insurance against the risk of divorce. There are two ways to reply to this point. First, the size of the maintenance payment is related to the former husband's earnings, whereas the extent of the woman's human capital depreciation is totally neglected. The ex-wife receives a certain fraction of his earnings but she is not compensated for the loss in marketable human capital that resulted from her staying home and that has a long-reaching impact on her future income potential. Second, maintenance payments in Germany are subject to the employment status of the wife prior to divorce. Entitlements are much more favorable if the wife has been working at least some hours than if she has not worked (for pay) at all. This regulation even suggests another strategic element for supplying labor within marriage.

4.5 Further research

In this chapter on female employment I tried to present a first step towards an econometric implementation of a dynamic bargaining model of family decision making. There are several directions in which this line of research could be profitably extended.

First, joint estimation of both the participation equation and an hours worked equation is desirable. One might attempt a procedure that controls for the selectivity bias of participation: From the probit estimates the inverse Mills ratio λ of participation could be computed and added to an OLS wage equation for workers only. Fitted values for wage rates derived from the selectivity bias-corrected wage equation estimates (step 4) together with the predicted conflict payoffs would be included in an additional step: an OLS regression on hours worked, again based on the restricted sample of employed women only (step 5). Thus the final labor supply estimation would then use two (sets of) imputed variables, the virtual wage rate and the virtual conflict payoff. However, preliminary results from an application of this procedure revealed severe multi-collinearity problems when using fitted conflict payoffs together with fitted wage rates as explaining variables in the hours equation. Further research should be dedicated to better empirical modeling of the participation decision to get around the collinearity problems.

Second, better estimates of the divorce probability are needed to be able to derive reliable selectivity corrections for the estimation of conflict payoffs. This is a problem of data constraints. A more detailed variable set including a wide range of questions on this subject would enable us to estimate labor supply with both selectivity corrected wage rates and selectivity corrected conflict payoffs. The selection rules of participation and divorce could then be controlled.

Given high unemployment rates and little variation of working hours, particularly those of men, one could doubt the observed labor force participation to be solely driven by supply side decisions. An extension of this analysis should therefore also consider demand side restrictions and their effects on family labor supply.[45]

Finally the results could be confirmed (or possibly rejected) by applying panel econometric techniques. In a panel estimation with fixed or random individual-specific effects one could test whether bargaining positions still matter for the employment decision once individual heterogeneity is controlled for.

Coming back to the theoretical model one would expect adverse selection to take place in the marriage market. Since high qualified women will suffer most from an intrafamily specialization according to traditional gender roles, that is, they are mostly at risk to get exploited within the family hold-up situation, they are also most likely to select into the group of singles. Women with lower educational levels, on the contrary, are not that much at risk to loose human capital during a family period. Hence, they are expected to constitute a greater share of the married group with children. The empirical evidence of an intrafamily bargaining argument to supply labor is not that much affected by this selection, though, since the strategic incentive will even be

45 See for example Grammig (1996).

underestimated by not considering those women who choose to remain single and thereby avoid the hold-up problem.

5 A panel-econometric analysis of the division of housework time

BÜRGERLICHES GESETZBUCH (GERMAN CIVIL CODE), §1354 until 1958:

Dem Manne steht die Entscheidung in allen das gemeinschaftliche eheliche Leben betreffenden Angelegenheiten zu.

(The husband is entitled to decide on all joint family matters.)

5.1 Introduction

In this chapter[46] the time use decisions of German couples are described and analyzed. Particular emphasis is given to the division of housework time between spouses depending on household structure. The empirical results are directly comparable with those of a study of U.S. families conducted by Joni Hersch and Leslie S. Stratton (1994). The gender-specific household activity data analyzed by Hersch and Stratton were taken from the Michigan Panel Study of Income Dynamics (PSID). Hersch and Stratton examined the time pattern, in particular the time devoted to household tasks, of more than 6,000 white American couples during the years 1979 to 1987. They restricted their sample to married dual earning couples with from ages 20 to 64, i.e. only the time use data of families in which *both* spouses are employed were included.

To explore the division of housework in Germany, similar data from the German Socio-Economic Panel (GSOEP)[47] covering the years from 1985 to 1994 are analyzed here. As an individual household microdata panel the GSOEP is roughly comparable with the PSID in both scope and design. As

[46] This chapter is a revised and extended version of Beblo (1998).

[47] For a detailed description of the GSOEP see Wagner et al. (1993) and Projektgruppe Sozio-oekonomisches Panel (1995).

for the analysis of individual time use the GSOEP is an even richer data source, having more detailed questions at the individual level (the PSID only provides answers from the husband on his own time use and that of his wife).

Apart from investigating German families' time allocation decisions the present study extends Hersch and Stratton's work in two respects. First, a non-cooperative bargaining hypothesis is derived and second, the panel structure of the data is exploited by controlling for individual-specific effects in estimation.

The division of housework in Germany looks very similar to what has been found for the U.S. On average men perform 20% of a family's total housework and 30% of its child care, a proportion that is almost independent of actual household circumstances (such as whether the wife works full-time or part-time). The empirical results show that husbands spend less time on household activities, the higher their relative wage earnings and the number of hours in paid work. This is what conventional time allocation theory predicts. Further, gender-specific household activity is also influenced by the age difference between spouses that may be interpreted as an indicator of a strategic advantage in family decision making in favor of the older spouse. This finding supports the "dominance argument" that the "home chores gap" (i.e. the difference in time spent on housework) between husband and wife is greater, the larger their age difference.

This chapter begins with a descriptive analysis of the time use of working couples in the GSOEP as related to different household characteristics. Next two competing theoretical approaches to intrafamily time allocation are briefly reviewed: the traditional time allocation theory, based on the unitary model of the household as a single decision-making unit, and a non-cooperative bargaining model that explicitly treats family members as distinct decision making units with potentially different preferences. The latter approach incorporates the existence of "dominance" as a strategic advantage in family decision making.

Following the theoretical discussion a panel-econometric analysis of intrafamily time allocation is undertaken. To investigate whether the division of housework can be explained by factors identified in the competing approaches, a three-regression model is estimated using the pooled GSOEP sample: one regression for time contributed to housework by each of the partners as well as a regression for the husband's share of housework time. Next the approach of Hersch and Stratton is extended to allow for fixed and random individual effects. In this way we may control for unobserved individual-specific characteristics. Due to the inclusion of time-invariant variables such as education and the age difference between partners, a mixed specification appears to best fit the data. Therefore both fixed individual-specific effects as well as random individual-specific factors are accounted for following a procedure suggested by Hsiao (1989). Thus, the better fit of the fixed-effects specification that allows for individual dummy variables together with the greater analytical potential of the random effects specification that uses time-invariant variables are incorporated into the estimation of housework time using "mixed effects". The chapter concludes with a summary of the empirical findings along with implications for the modeling of intrafamily time allocation.

5.2 The time use of employed couples

The empirical results in this paper are based on time use data from the West German subsample of the GSOEP, encompassing ten waves over the time period from 1985 to 1994 (with the exception of the year 1990[48]). The analysis is restricted to married couples where both spouses have paid jobs. It is further limited to adults between the ages of 20 and 60 to prevent the results from being excessively affected by retirement behavior.

The time use data are based on the following question that husbands and wives were each asked separately:

"How does your typical (work-)day look like? How many hours do you spend on the following activities?

- *occupation (including multiple jobs and commuting time),*
- *housework and shopping,*
- *child care,*
- *repairs at the house or the car and garden work,*
- *education,*
- *TV, Video,*
- *Hobbies and other leisure activities"*

Table 5.1 summarizes the respondents' answers broken down by different household characteristics. The sample is restricted to individuals who did not report more than 24 hours per activity. Double counting of multiple activities may still occur as seems obvious, for instance when making errands and taking the children at the same time. Actual double counting, however, appears to be of subordinate importance, as can be seen with the cumulated means of Table 5.1 (11.99 hours total for the average man and 13.08 hours for the average woman. These numbers still allow for a residual amount of time for

[48] No data from wave G of the GSOEP have been used since time use questions in that year differed from other years.

other uses, most importantly leisure and personal care.). The final sample includes 1595 couples with 5183 observations.

Table 5.1: Average time use of employed spouses

		Hours spent per day		Male share
		Husband	Wife	
ALL OBSERVATIONS	n=5183			
Job		9.50	7.58	0.56
Housework		0.85	3.35	0.20
Child care		0.65	1.59	0.29
Repairs, garden		0.99	0.56	0.64
WITHOUT CHILDREN	n=2691			
Job		9.57	8.12	0.54
Housework		0.81	3.03	0.21
Child care		0.05	0.12	0.29
Repairs, garden		1.03	0.59	0.64
WITH CHILDREN	n=2492			
Job		9.43	7.00	0.57
Housework		0.90	3.70	0.20
Child care		1.30	3.18	0.29
Repairs, garden		0.96	0.53	0.64
WIFE WORKING FULL-TIME	n=3533			
Job		9.46	8.79	0.52
Housework		0.87	2.87	0.23
Child care		0.60	1.16	0.34
Repairs, garden		0.95	0.45	0.68

Data source: German Socio-Economic Panel, 1985-94 (excluding 1990)

Married men dedicate an average of 9.5 hours a day to their jobs and 1.5 hours to the household activities, child care and housework. Their working wives, on the contrary, carry out about 7.6 hours paid work outside the home relative to nearly 5 hours of unpaid housework and child care. The husband's share of these household activities in the total sample amounts to hardly more than 23%.

In a comparison of different sub-samples, such as couples without children under 16 living in the household, families with children and households where the wife has full-time employment, deviations can be noticed only with respect to her time use. Husbands' proportionate household production remains 20% and only increases to 23% when wives have full-time employment. But even then, the average job-working time of the wife is still 40 minutes less than her husband's, whereas her housework is three times greater than his and her child care time is double. Despite having full-time employment, this indicates not only a greater overall time burden for the wife (i.e. less leisure time) but also the implicit specialization of men and women according to traditional gender-specific responsibilities.

Women with children not only devote more time to actually looking after their children but also take over a greater share of other household tasks. At the same time they cut back their employment by one hour. As a result, their daily work load sums up to 14.4 hours (including gardening etc.), which is about two hours more than their husbands' total work time[49]. Whereas the presence of children results in a visible effect on the daily time pattern of a woman, it has only a marginal impact on the time use of a man. His time use only changes with regard to child care time, not with regard to the accompanying greater workload in the household. In spite of the increasing female employment and the dissolving gender-specific division of paid work, family work still remains the responsibility and sphere of action of the woman of the house.

Overall male time use stays relatively constant, seemingly independent of different household characteristics. The time use of women, on the contrary, forms the flexible factor in adjusting to the varying demand of family work. Also, the total work load (paid and unpaid labor together) shows a greater variation for women than for men according to family structure and employment status. In general men have more disposable time than women. The same conclusion was drawn by the Federal Statistical Office when making a representative study on the time use of the German population[50]. The more a woman engages in (paid) work the greater is the leisure gap between herself and her partner, since husbands do not seem to adjust their time allocation to their wife's employment status. [51]

---

[49] Time spent on repairs and gardening as particularly male dominated time uses will not be included in the housework-time measure, though, due to the qualitative difference between these tasks that are performed infrequently (and where in most cases the timing is not fixed) versus everyday duties that are more or less inevitable such as changing a baby's diapers.

[50] In this survey every family member above the age of 12 was asked to report about his or her daily time pattern (see Statistisches Bundesamt 1995).

[51] Or, as Arlie Hochschild states in her book on *The second shift* (1989): The wage differential between men and women on the labor market is reflected in a leisure

A comparison with the American study conducted by Hersch and Stratton shows remarkable similarities: In both countries there are large disparities in time spent on housework between husbands and wives. The difference between male and female participation in family work increases with the presence of children in the household. It decreases slightly when the wife holds a full-time employment. The relative share contributed by American men ranges from 25 to 29%. German husbands take over 20 to 23% of the total housework. When taking into account child care time, the male share in Germany further increases another four percentage points.

An important qualification to the empirical findings needs to be noted here: The time use data from the GSOEP are generally not regarded as the most accurate data source for time use studies. This is partly due to the non-standardized treatment of multiple activities within the GSOEP. In comparison with the data from a time-use study by the German Federal Statistical Office in 1991/92, however, where multiple activities (main activity and additional activities) were explicitly accounted for and respondents had to report their daily schedule in intervals of five-minute length, averages for the two data sets do not show any serious deviations. In particular, the relationship between average time use of men and average time use of women on different activities is of same magnitude. It is interesting to note that the respondents within the GSOEP answered questions regarding their time use as though they were asked for their main activity. This becomes particularly clear with the numbers on child care time: When asked about their main activity by the statistical office, employed husbands reported 40 minutes spent on child care daily, employed wives reported 1.5 hours (Statistisches Bundesamt 1995). These numbers are nearly identical with those from the GSOEP.

5.3 Theoretical approaches to intrafamily time allocation

Various economic approaches have attempted to explain the individual choice of time use and the division of labor within a household setting. The first approach to modeling time allocation decisions was made by Gary S. Becker (1965) in his pioneering contribution to the New Home Economics. This approach was later extended by Reuben Gronau (1973, 1977). Whereas Becker confined his model to the decision between household production and market work, Gronau took account of the three time uses: market work, housework, and leisure. Within this unitary framework both spouses specialize according to their comparative advantages across competing time uses.

---

gap between spouses. Men concentrate on their occupational responsibilities, whereas women manage a first shift at the paid job plus an additional unpaid second shift at home for their families.

Thus, a higher male wage rate automatically leads to the well-known gender-specific division of work. Discrimination of women in the labor market, as manifested in poorer promotion prospects or lower wages, will also contribute to specialization, even with equal educational backgrounds of husband and wife. Furthermore, the mere ability of women to bear children as well as the complementarity between the bearing and rearing of children establishes a female comparative advantage in household activities, according to Becker (1981a: 21f). In this context the division of labor within families is seen as having a biological determinant as well. Since in this unitary model the household is treated like a single-decision making unit, different preferences of husband and wife, in particular the existence of dominance or power within the household, are ignored[52].

Modeling intrafamily decision making as a non-cooperative bargaining game provides a more promising approach as it provides an explanation for the gender-specific division of labor by means of a dominance argument. In this chapter I will focus on the non-cooperative bargaining model of Kristian Bolin (1996, 1997) that explains the unequal division of family work as the outcome of a Stackelberg game between the spouses[53]. In this model husband and wife both maximize the consumption of two goods, a private good that is paid for by individual labor income and a public family good that is generated by household production. Even if the product "housework and child care" is only provided by one spouse, as a public good it will be consumed by the other partner as well. Now, being a Stackelberg leader the first mover can decide on his or her time allocation first. In particular he or she fixes the own provision of the family good and, thus, sets the restrictions for the time use decision of the partner[54].

Due to traditional norms or initial resource distribution men are more likely to have a first mover advantage than women. Dominance or power as a strategic advantage may also arise out of an age difference between spouses. In

[52] In Chapter 2 the unitary model is explained in more detail.

[53] Susan Fleck (1996) applies a similar model to explain the labor force participation of women in Honduras. By means of a non-cooperative bargaining model she includes power as the control over decision making which leads to an asymmetry within the household regarding time use decisions and the distribution of surplus created in the household. Kai Konrad and Kjell Erik Lommerud (1995) also model the family as a non-cooperative game in which both spouses decide on the supply of a family public good. Treating husband and wife as equals, however, they use a Cournot game with simultaneous decision making.

[54] The unequal division of housework time might also be interpreted as the outcome of a cooperative bargaining game with asymmetric bargaining weights assigned to the household members. These bargaining weights would then be determined by the spouses' relative power or, following Elizabeth Katz's (1997) argumentation, their respective "voices" in the decision making process.

the typical case, with the husband older than his wife (3 years on average in the sample) he has a headstart in deciding about his labor force participation and the other time uses. In terms of intrafamily time allocation he acts, whereas his wife can only react, given the chosen place of residence and place of work of her husband; in other words, given his time use and his contribution to household production. Apart from any comparative advantages, dominance within a family leads to a specialization in paid labor of the dominating spouse and the provision of the family good by the dominated spouse. This non-cooperative setting offers the advantage of allowing us to distinguish the empirical results drawn from the game theoretic approach from those of the human capital model. This is accomplished by using the age difference between husband and wife as a proxy for dominance within the household, i.e. as an indicator variable for a strategic advantage in family decision making.[55]

5.4 The division of housework time: estimation results

To investigate whether the division of housework can be explained by factors identified in the competing theoretical approaches, a three-regression model has been estimated using the data set described above: one regression for time contributed to housework by each of the partners as well as one regression for the husband's share of housework time.[56] According to the study conducted by Hersch and Stratton, first, the linear relationship between the husband's share of total housework time and various individual and household variables is estimated as a reflection of the actual intrafamily time allocation decision. In the second and third regression the respective amounts of housework time of husband and wife are examined as dependent variables. This procedure allows us to decompose the impact on the husband's share into the impacts on female or male time use separately.

First the three-regression model is estimated using the pooled GSOEP sample. The results are presented and compared with the American findings. Extending the approach of Hersch and Stratton, individual-specific effects are then allowed for. To exploit the panel structure of the data set, a fixed effects

---

[55] A point could be made concerning the possible endogeneity of the matching process. As long as younger women are observed marrying older men, they are somehow choosing dominating partners of their own free will. The ideal model, therefore, would have to explain family formation and time use decisions simultaneously. To hold the analysis manageable we will restrict our study to intrafamily time allocation.

[56] To make the empirical results directly comparable with those of the American study only housework time was used as the independent variable. However, additional sensitivity tests with regard to time spent on child care were performed. The resulting effects were substantively unchanged.

specification, a random effects specification and, finally, a mixed specification are estimated in turn.

Which are the factors identified by the competing theoretical approaches? As for the traditional theory, only the impact of variables that Hersch and Stratton derived from the unitary model are investigated to make the empirical results directly comparable between the countries. As for the non-cooperative approach, an additional dominance indicator is identified.

According to the Beckerian theory, the husband's contribution to the household's total labor income should show a negative effect on the husband's share as well as the absolute amount of his housework. A positive impact is predicted on the wife's activity using the comparative-advantage argument. The same conclusion, though for different reasons, can be drawn out of the non-cooperative dominance theory. Since the man as the first mover chooses paid work over unpaid housework, one should observe less male household activity the higher the intrafamily wage differential.

With regard to total household income, again the same signs are expected from both theories. This is also true for time spent in the job. Because of substitution of home produced goods with purchased market goods total household income is supposed to be negatively correlated with the housework time of both spouses, while more hours contributed to an occupation might be accompanied by less own family work but more family work provided by the partner.

Educational level, on the other hand, may have differing effects on household production. A higher level of human capital combined with a comparative advantage in market work and a better bargaining position within the family might suggest an inverse relation between a partner's years of schooling and the hours devoted to housework. It then predicts a positive relationship between own schooling and the other spouse's amount of housework.[57]

The presence of children (measured as a dummy variable) is presumed to be positively related to total family work hours. This being due to the increase in opportunity costs of market work and due to the increase in the value of household activity. Following the comparative-advantage argument, we expect the mother to specialize in housework and thus expand her family work hours whereas the father pulls back.

Finally, two age-based variables have been used to account for cohort effects as well as the dominance effect: The average of the husband's and wife's ages provides a control for changes in attitudes and social norms regarding

[57] Though a higher educational level might also have a positive impact on an equal division of family labor among husband and wife due to attitudinal changes. This second effect might offset the human capital one.

the household division of labor and gender roles. Therefore, the younger a couple, the more equal sharing of family work between the spouses one expects, ceteris paribus. At the same time, the lower the average age of a couple the greater the probability of children living in the household and thus the more family work to do. As with the education variable these are contrary effects which leave the resulting sign undetermined. Regarding the dominance effect the age difference between husband and wife is included to serve as an indicator for a first-mover advantage in intrafamily time allocation decisions. It provides a test of the empirical relevance of the non-cooperative dominance argument. The larger the age difference between the spouses the smaller the amount of housework expected by the first mover (husband) and the higher the contribution expected by the follower (wife).

5.4.1 Pooled sample

In an unbalanced least-squares regression of the pooled sample several statistical interdependencies can be seen (Table 5.2). The higher the husband's share of labor income and the more hours spent on his job, the lower his contribution to household production. As expected, the underlying partial effects are a reduction of male housework accompanied by an increase in female household activity. With rising total household income both spouses devote less time to housework and child care. The husband's relative share, however, still decreases. At high income levels the basic family activities are increasingly the wife's responsibility.

A rise in male employment has a statistically significant effect on the absolute amount of family work supplied by both partners. The result is a lower relative contribution by men. In contrast, female employment is positively related to the husband's share.

Each additional year of schooling significantly increases men's relative household activity by 0.4% or 0.8%, for men and women, respectively. While the wife reduces her housework time, her husband takes over more family activities. As for female education this observation is consistent with both the specialization argument by Becker and the dominance argument by Bolin. As for male education this might be interpreted as an indication for assortative matching on the marriage market. That is, men with a higher educational level tend to marry women with high level of human capital and, thus, specialization advantages within the household are reduced. An alternative explanation would be that of attitudinal differences towards a gender-based division of work in the family depending on the educational background of household members.

Table 5.2: OLS coefficient estimates of the pooled sample

	Husband's share housework time		Hours housework, husband		Hours housework, wife	
	Coeff. est.	(Stand. dev.)	Coeff. est.	(Stand. dev.)	Coeff. est.	(Stand. dev.)
Husband's share of wage income	-.108	(.024)	-.369	(.122)	1.73	(.205)
Household income/1000	-.003	(.001)	-.029	(.006)	-.045	(.010)
Hours paid work, husband	-.017	(.001)	-.082	(.007)	.029	(.012)
Hours paid work, wife	.011	(.001)	.017	(.007)	-.202	(.011)
Education, husband	.004	(.001)	.009	(.007)	-.037	(.012)
Education, wife	.008	(.001)	.013	(.008)	-.064	(.013)
Child dummy	-.023	(.006)	.081	(.029)	.486	(.048)
Age average	-.003	(.000)	-.005	(.002)	.028	(.003)
Age difference	-.002	(.001)	-.010	(.003)	.004	(.006)
Constant	.345	(.031)	1.798	(.160)	3.447	(.269)
Adjusted R^2	.10		.04		.23	

Data source: German Socio-Economic Panel, 1985-94 (excluding 1990).

The presence of children in the household (as captured in a dummy variable for children under 16 living in the household) decreases the male share by 2%. This is because mothers expand their household activities to a higher proportion when a child is to be cared for.

The older the spouse the lower the male share of household activity. With each additional year the share falls by 0.3 percentage points. Thus the German data suggest, even more than the results of Hersch and Stratton for the U.S., that men take over an increasing share of the family work in younger couples. This is consistent with changing attitudes and an evolution away from traditional gender roles. Nonetheless these data show that Hersch and Stratton's vision of diminishing gender differences in work histories and housework time paired with greater equality in the allocation of housework is not exactly around the corner.

Age difference as an indicator for dominance, on the other hand, reveals a statistically significant inverse relation with the husband's contribution to housework, the important prediction from the non-cooperative model: The larger the age difference between husband and wife the higher their home chores gap, other things equal. Each additional year between the husband's and the wife's ages reduces male housework time by 40 seconds (starting from an average of 51 minutes) whereas the reaction in female hours has a positive coefficient but is not statistically significant.

This is a rather small effect of the dominance indicator, identified by the non-cooperative bargaining approach. Nevertheless, it is a statistically significant one with regard to the husband's relative contribution and it leads to a slightly better fit of the model. When including the age difference as an additional regressor in the regression equation of the husband's share of household activities the adjusted R^2 improves from 10.0% to 10.2%. When estimating the husband's total housework hours the R^2 increases from 4.0% to 4.2%. Only with regard to female housework time the age difference between the spouses hardly alters the fit of the regression model.

In spite of all the differences between the American and the German study - different time periods as well as country-specific differences in culture, political background, labor markets - to a large extent the GSOEP data show the same patterns as the PSID numbers (for a summary comparison of the American and German estimation results see Table A in the Appendix).

5.4.2 Fixed effects

Up to now the analysis has been solely based on the pooled panel data set. Yet, individual preferences or characteristics and household structures do make a difference in a person's use of time, especially with regard to the question of child care. Extending the approach of Hersch and Stratton we can allow for these unobservable individual-specific aspects of family work. In a panel data analysis these are controlled for with fixed individual effects. Introducing dummy variables for every single respondent we are able to take into account differences between the respondents that are due to omitted but time invarying factors. For individual i in period t the model can be formulated as

$$(5.1) \qquad y_{it} = \mu + \beta' x_{it} + \alpha_i + u_{it}, \quad i = 1,\dots,N, \quad t = 1,\dots,T,$$

where μ and α_i are fixed constants, μ being the mean intercept and α_i representing the individual deviation from the common mean. The mean zero normally distributed random error term u_{it} represents the effects of the omitted variables that are peculiar to both the individual units and time periods. Estimation of the fixed effects model yields the least-squares dummy-variable estimator β that is determined by the variation within the data of each individual. This way the direct effects on housework time from all other variables can be isolated.

An F-test for the equality of all individual effects is conducted (Judge et al. 1988). As the rejection of the null hypothesis shows (Table 5.3), the heterogeneity of the sample needs to be taken into account in order to obtain efficient estimation results.

Table 5.3: Fixed effects regression

	Husband's share housework time		Hours housework, husband		Hours housework, wife	
	Coeff. est.	(Stand. dev.)	Coeff. est.	(Stand. dev.)	Coeff. est.	(Stand. dev.)
Husband's share of wage income	-.136	(.041)	-.361	(.224)	2.111	(.365)
Household income/1000	-.003	(.001)	-.017	(.007)	-.032	(.012)
Hours paid work, husband	-.007	(.002)	-.031	(.010)	.025	(.016)
Hours paid work, wife	.004	(.002)	-.006	(.093)	-.138	(.015)
Child dummy	.010	(.010)	.123	(.057)	.300	(.093)
Age average	.046	(.015)	.094	(.084)	-.100	(.137)
Education, husband	-		-		-	
Education, wife	-		-		-	
Age difference	-		-		-	
Adjusted R^2	.41		.31		.47	
F-test p	.000	(2.80)	.000	(2.28)	.000	(2.61)

Data source: German Socio-Economic Panel, 1985-94 (excluding 1990).

A fixed effects estimator requires within-group variation of all variables. Since education and birth years do not vary in time, at least not in the observed sample of already employed adults, the corresponding variables could not be included in the fixed-effects regression. Thus, only a reduced regression equation with time variant variables was estimated. Apart from this, the results were substantially unchanged in comparison with those of the pooled estimation. In particular the signs of most coefficient estimates did not change. This is true except for the couple's age average which reveals a positive impact on the husband's total amount and his share of housework time once individual-specific effects are included in the regression (only the second shows statistical significance at the 5%-level). In other words, even allowing for unobserved fixed individual-specific characteristics, the relationship between housework by gender and income, time use and opportunity cost variables remains a statistically significant one.

More crucially, accounting for individual effects leads to an improvement of the statistical power of the estimation. Whereas in the pooled model only 10% (4% and 23%, respectively) of the variance could be explained by the regression equation, now the adjusted R^2 amounts to 0.41 or even 0.47 when regarding total housework time of the wife. These numbers point out the appropriateness of a fixed-effects specification.

5.4.3 Random effects

In contrast to a fixed-effects specification, in a panel data model with random effects, individual-specific factors are regarded as independent random variables. Thus, the sample examined is viewed as a random draw of the whole population such that the individual differences represent the characteristics of the total population and are not correlated with any other regressors. The residual v_{it} is assumed to consist of two components:

$$(5.2) \qquad v_{it} = \alpha_i + u_{it}, \quad i = 1,...,N, \qquad t = 1,...,T,$$

where α_i represents the random individual-specific effect with mean zero and variance σ_α^2 and u_{it} represents the residual effect of omitted variables with mean zero and variance σ_u^2.

The resulting coefficient estimates do not differ substantially from those of the pooled sample (Table 5.4). The Lagrange-multiplier test, as the F-test before, supports controlling for individual-specific factors when testing for random-coefficient variation among individuals.

The random effects model only explains the same share of the sample variance as the pooled model does though. Since the null hypothesis of the Hausman Test for the equality of the dummy variable estimator and the generalized least squares estimator is rejected, the fixed-coefficient model should be used. Furthermore, the assumption of individual effects as being random or fixed depends on whether inferences are made unconditional on population characteristics or whether they are instead conditional on individual characteristics. Since in this analysis we are looking at a specific sub-sample consisting of working couples only, a panel analysis with fixed individual effects seems to provide the appropriate framework for analyzing time allocation decisions within these households. However, sweeping out one of the most interesting variables, the age difference between husband and wife, no longer allows us to test the empirical relevance of the dominance argument.

Table 5.4: Random effects regression

	Husband's share housework time		Hours housework, husband		Hours housework, wife	
	Coeff. est.	(Stand. dev.)	Coeff. est.	(Stand. dev.)	Coeff. est.	(Stand. dev.)
Husband's share of wage income	-.143	(.026)	-.467	(.135)	2.011	(.221)
Household income/1000	-.003	(.001)	-.027	(.006)	-.034	(.090)
Hours paid work, husband	-.013	(.001)	-.069	(.007)	.035	(.011)
Hours paid work, wife	.008	(.001)	.012	(.007)	-.173	(.011)
Education, husband	.003	(.002)	.005	(.009)	-.027	(.017)
Education, wife	.008	(.002)	.013	(.009)	-.065	(.019)
Child dummy	-.018	(.006)	.083	(.033)	.439	(.056)
Age average	-.003	(.000)	-.005	(.002)	.030	(.003)
Age difference	-.001	(.000)	-.008	(.004)	-.003	(.008)
Constant	.357	(.036)	1.810	(.181)	2.870	(.324)
Adjusted R^2	.10		.04		.23	
LM-test p	.000	(1245)	.000	(852)	.000	(574)
Hausman-test p	.000	(47)	.000	(42)	.000	(35)

Data source: German Socio-Economic Panel, 1985-94 (excluding 1990).

5.4.4 Mixed specification

Due to time-invariant variables such as education and age difference that are dropped from the fixed effects estimation, a mixed specification appears to best fit the data. Following a procedure proposed by Hsiao (1989: 50ff), those variables that vary across individual units but do not vary over time (education variables, age difference) are collected together in a vector z_i' that is accompanied by random individual-specific effects. Other variables that do vary over time (working hours, income variables, child dummy, age average) are included as regressors X_i, varying with fixed individual-specific effects (e is a vector of ones):

$$y_i = e\mu + ez_i'\gamma + X_i\beta + e\alpha_i + u_i, \quad i = 1,\ldots,N. \tag{5.3}$$

In a first step Ordinary Least Squares (OLS) estimation is applied to a fixed effects specification with time variant variables only ($Q = I_T - 1/T \cdot ee'$ is the transformation matrix):

$$(5.4) \qquad Qy_i = QX_i\beta + Qu_i, \quad i = 1,\dots,N.$$

Using the dummy-variable estimator $\hat{\beta}$, estimates for γ and μ are obtained in the second step by regressing the individual means over time on all time-invariant variables:

$$(5.5) \qquad \bar{y}_i - \bar{x}_i'\hat{\beta} = \mu + z_i'\gamma + \alpha_i + \bar{u}_i, \quad i = 1,\dots,N,$$

where the α_i are assumed random. The explicit incorporation of time-invariant variables helps to reduce the correlation between the fixed constants and all other explanatory variables.

The estimation results of this two-step procedure, presented in Table 5.5, show that the age difference still has a statistically significant effect on the division of housework between husband and wife in explaining the wife's contribution to housework time[58]. Economically speaking, the larger the age gap between the spouses and, thus, the more pronounced the first-mover advantage of the husband, the greater is the home chores gap predicted by the dominance argument.

Even though the estimates of the mixed specification do not differ substantially in sign and in magnitude from those of the pooled model[59], it incorporates both the better fit of the fixed-effects specification by allowing for individual dummy variables and the greater analytical potential of the random effects specification by including time-invariant variables.

---

[58] At this point it should be noted that, if the individual-specific effect α_i is correlated with the time constant variables z_i, the OLS estimates of γ and μ will be inconsistent and a more elaborate procedure suggested by Hausman and Taylor (1981) will have to be applied. For this reason the T-statistic might not provide reliable values to be able to reject the Null-hypothesis of no relationship between the regressors and the respective housework hours. The signs of the coefficients for age difference, however, still support the findings of the pooled and the random regression.

[59] Exception: The presence of a child now increases the husband's share of family activity by 1% which is due to a slight convergence of the partial effects.

Table 5.5: "Mixed effects" regression

	Husband's share housework time		Hours house-work, husband		Hours house-work, wife	
	Coeff. est.	(Stand. dev.)	Coeff. est.	(Stand. dev.)	Coeff. est.	(Stand. dev.)
Step 1: Fixed effects						
Husband's share of wage income	-.136	(.041)	-.361	(.224)	2.112	(.365)
Household income/1000	-.003	(.001)	-.017	(.009)	-.032	(.012)
Hours paid work, husband	-.007	(.002)	-.031	(.010)	.025	(.016)
Hours paid work, wife	.004	(.002)	-.006	(.093)	-.138	(.015)
Child dummy	.010	(.010)	.123	(.057)	.298	(.093)
Age average	.046	(.015)	.094	(.084)	-.100	(.137)
Adjusted R^2	.41		.31		.47	
Step 2: Random effects						
Education, husband	-.0002	(.0003)	.0016	(.0005)	-.0027	(.0014)
Education, wife	-.0002	(.0003)	-.0027	(.0005)	.0005	(.0015)
Age difference	-.0002	(.0001)	-.0001	(.0002)	.0024	(.0007)
Constant	.0037	(.0029)	.0065	(.0048)	.0179	(.0146)
Adjusted R^2	.0002		.0050		.0030	

Data source: German Socio-Economic Panel, 1985-94 (excluding 1990).

5.5 Conclusions

We may summarize the empirical results as follows: If there is anything as an empirical law in intrafamily time allocation, then it appears to be the amount of time husbands devote to household production and work in the labor market and hence also their amount of leisure time. Regardless of actual household characteristics, men perform 20% of a family's total housework and 30% of its child care activity. A flexible adjustment to differing family circumstances is exclusively provided by the wife's time use, namely, her leisure time. The observed gap between gender-specific responsibilities or time inputs is a phenomenon which cannot be fully explained by the traditional theory of time allocation. Non-cooperative bargaining approaches, namely the dominance models of Bolin and Fleck, provide an appropriate framework for answering these kinds of questions.

The econometric results of this paper indicate that gender-specific household activity is not solely influenced by factors identified in the Beckerian time allocation theory such as human capital and the opportunity costs of market work. Even allowing for husbands spending less time on household activities as a consequence of higher relative wage earnings and more hours dedicated to the labor market, gender-specific household activity is still influenced by the age difference between spouses that may be interpreted as an indicator for a strategic advantage in family decision making in favor of the older spouse. This finding supports the dominance argument that the home chores gap between husband and wife grows with their age difference. The result holds even when allowing for both fixed and random individual-specific effects within a mixed specification framework.

The size of the age difference effect is thus a rather small one, suggesting an inherent Stackelberg advantage of the husband in family decision making (particularly with respect to time use), just as the quoted German civil law at the beginning of this chapter states: "The husband is entitled to decide on all joint family matters." This law has already been abolished in 1958, yet the underlying gender roles seem rather persistent.

5.6 Appendix

Table 5.A: Comparison of American and German estimation results (pooled samples)

	Husband's share of housework time	
	GSOEP	PSID
Husband's share of wage income	-	-
Total household income	-	-
Time spent on the job, husband	-	-
Time spent on the job, wife	+	+
Education, husband	+	+
Education, wife	+	[+]
Child dummy	-	[+]
Age/Cohort effect	-	-
Age difference	-	
Constant	+	+
Adj. R^2	.10	.12

Data source: German Socio-Economic Panel, 1985-1994 (excluding 1990), own estimation results. PSID, 1979-1987 (excluding 1982), estimation results of Hersch/Stratton (1994).
Note: Positive signs indicate positive correlation and significance at the 5%-level, negative signs indicate inverse correlation and significance at the 5%-level. Signs in brackets indicate no significance at the 5%-level.

6 Leisure - A model on private provision of family public goods

6.1 Introduction

The United Nations *Human Development Report's* review of time use in 31 countries in 1995 documents the fact that women consistently enjoy less leisure time than men with women working longer hours (paid and unpaid) than men in nearly every country. In a German time budget survey for 1991/92 the overall leisure gap between men and women amounts to more than 20 minutes on an average day (Statistisches Bundesamt 1995). When it comes to working adults the gender-specific difference increases to more than half an hour for those in full-time jobs. Half an hour may seem a small amount of time, but it is worthwhile noting that it took several decades for contracted daily working time to fall by this amount.

The observation that an employed man enjoys more leisure than his working wife is generally attributed to different wage rates of men and women, whether due to differing levels of human capital or due to labor market discrimination against women. On average, men are still paid about a third more than women. With variations across different branches and occupations this earnings gap has been decreasing very slowly over the last decades, but remains consistently significant (Statistisches Bundesamt 1998b).

The relation between the wage gap and the leisure gap has been widely debated in social science research. A sociological approach, represented by Joan Huber and Glenna Spitze (1983) and later extended by Arlie Hochschild (1989), sees family time use arrangements as much a cultural phenomenon as they are economic. By analyzing a sample of employed couples drawn from a larger national study by the University of Michigan in 1981 Hochschild found that women did more housework the less they earned relative to their husbands. But even if they had higher labor incomes than their husbands, they still performed "their" household tasks and did not enjoy increased leisure.

Low-earning women, in comparison, increased their leisure time by working shorter hours.

Hochschild concluded “that the leisure gap between wives and husbands reflects something more than these couples’ pragmatic adaptation to the higher wages of American men - an interplay of gender strategy” (Hochschild 1989: 278). She interpreted this behavior as following the principle of balancing: wives who out-earn their husbands compensate them for their “loss of face” by not delegating more household work. This finding is supported by a study of Brines (1994) who argues that an economically dependent husband does less housework the more he depends on his wife for income. Established domestic gender roles imply that once a man’ financial identity as the breadwinner has been undermined he cannot afford to further weaken his position by doing housework (see also Daly 1996).

The economic theory of time allocation was initiated by Gary Becker (1965, 1976). In Becker’s theory a couple maximizes (joint) utility when both partners allocate their time according to their comparative productivity advantages. That is, if the husband has a higher wage than his wife he will specialize in paid employment and she will specialize in household production, while possibly holding a part-time job. The higher the wage differential the greater the difference between the amounts of time the man and the woman spend at home[60]. Since Becker did not distinguish home time between household work and leisure, no direct link between wages and the *leisure gap* can be drawn.

In recent years, more sophisticated game-theoretic models have been developed where the husband and the wife interact as individual family members. The seminal papers by Marilyn Manser and Murray Brown (1980) and Marjorie McElroy and Mary Jean Horney (1981) propose a Nash bargaining model where divorce or remaining single are possible threat points. Shelly Lundberg and Robert Pollak (1993) consider the case where the threat point is not divorce but a non-cooperative outcome within marriage. Kai Konrad and Kjell-Erik Lommerud (1995) explicitly model a non-cooperative game of private provision of a public good. In the emerging Nash equilibrium there is, in general, underprovision of the family public good. A similar approach is presented by Kristian Bolin (1996). His non-cooperative model explains the unequal division of family work as the outcome of a Stackelberg game between the spouses.

In most of these models husband and wife basically maximize the consumption of two goods, a private good that is paid for by individual labor income, and a public family good that is generated by household production. From this we cannot make predictions about different time uses at home. In other

[60] This specialization argument is presented in more detail in Chapter 2.

words, there is no distinction between time spent at home looking after children and time spent watching TV.

The aim of this approach is to model leisure in an *explicit* way[61]. Leisure is included as a private good in the model. Although it is sometimes difficult to establish whether a certain time use produces a public or a private good, let us assume that time spent in paid market labor and time spent in unpaid household labor both generate family public goods, to which both spouses contribute. Time spent in paid labor yields wage income that can be regarded as a family public good since housing, transportation or, generally, the family's living is purchased with that income. Time spent in unpaid labor also yields a public good to the family. Household production such as child care, a clean house and a nice garden are public goods privately provided by each partner.

Although modeling labor income as a joint public good is a very strong assumption, it may well be plausible to assume that this income has much more of a public good character than leisure. Leisure or private time is defined as time spent on self-determined activities. Since these are activities that are pursued for their own sake, they must be exclusively performed by that same person and cannot be delegated to anyone else and then transferred. This concept of leisure follows the *third person criterion* (see Schäfer/Schwarz 1996 and Ott 1999). Whereas labor refers to all activities that are inputs of a production process the output of which is interpersonally transferable, leisure does not yield any such outputs that could be traded in return for other services. Sport activities, watching TV or eating and sleeping, for instance, are considered leisure activities, since they have to be performed by oneself.

Thus we have a three-good model with three time uses: market work, household work and private leisure time. Following Bolin (1996), let us assume that the husband can choose his time allocation first to become the Stackelberg leader (the "Stackelberg husband") in a non-cooperative game. As in Chapter 5 it can be argued that men are more likely to have such a first mover advantage than women due to institutional and economic factors. Thus the model is formally related to Wolfgang Buchholz and co-authors (1997) who analyze a game of private provision of public goods when two individuals sequentially contribute to a public good. In contrast to their model with transferable income in this setting time cannot be transferred between partners.

In the Stackelberg game the husband decides on his provision of the public goods first and thereby sets the restrictions for the follower, his wife. By applying a Stackelberg game it turns out that even with equal wages for husband and wife, the husband generally enjoys more leisure due to his strategic

[61] This chapter is joint work with Julio Robledo. It is a revised and extended version of Beblo/Robledo (1999).

Stackelberg advantage. Since a couple's decision on who will be the main breadwinner is associated with such long term consequences, a non-cooperative framework better captures the full commitment character of this decision than a static cooperative game. Even if partners actually make a cooperative choice, the outcome of the non-cooperative game is interesting in itself, because it may provide the threat point of the cooperative game (as in Lundberg/Pollak 1993).

In this setting it will be investigated whether women who outearn their husbands (we assume an exogenously given wage rate) bear a double time burden of market work plus household work as described in the sociological literature. The static results confirm the sociological findings that there is more to a gender-specific leisure gap than the wage differential between women and men. Moreover, although not explicitly modeled, the approach provides an explanation why the wage inequality between women and men persists so stubbornly over time. Social structures that favor Stackelberg husbands lead to an intra-family time allocation that keeps women out of full-time employment, because that maximizes their leisure time. If part-time jobs are paid less (on an hourly base) than full-time occupations, the result will be a persisting wage gap.

The chapter proceeds as follows. In the next section the basic model is outlined. Section 6.3 analyzes the general Stackelberg game. The last section summarizes the main results.

6.2 The model

We consider a model of intrafamily time allocation in which each family member has to make his or her own time allocation and consumption decisions. Each partner's decision problem is interrelated with these individual choices, however, due to the provision of family public goods. Time T can be allocated among three main uses: paid market work g, unpaid household work h and leisure l.

The sole private good in this model is individual leisure time. Intrahousehold bargaining over the distribution of household resources therefore implies bargaining over individual time use, namely that time that can be disposed of freely by each partner. In this context, making a good bargain entails getting away with more leisure time which is the only good that can be consumed individually. Housing, child care etc., on the contrary, are consumed publicly. It is assumed that they are not associated with distributive conflicts between the partners. As a result, within such a setting it is the amount of leisure time that has to be referred to when analyzing outcomes of intrafamily bargaining.

The utility functions are given by:

$$U^m(h_m, h_f, g_m, g_f) = V(l_m) + G(w_m g_m + w_f g_f) + H(h_m, h_f)$$

and $$U^f(h_m, h_f, g_m, g_f) = V(l_f) + G(w_m g_m + w_f g_f) + H(h_m, h_f)$$

where G and H are the outputs of the public goods market and household work, respectively, and l_i, $i = m, f$ denotes the leisure time of the spouses. All three goods (leisure, market work and homework) are assumed to be normal goods. With the small letters g_f, h_f and g_m, h_m we denote her and his contributions to both public goods[62]. In our model it is irrelevant where the money income comes from: a dollar from his income is as valuable as a dollar earned by her: $G = G(w_m g_m + w_f g_f)$. This linearity in the contributions to money income allows for corner solutions where one partner might be the only money earner. The household production technology is more general, allowing for cross effects: $H = H(h_m, h_f)$.

The functions V and G are assumed to have positive but decreasing first derivatives. The household production function H has marginal productivities $H_{hm} > 0$ and $H_{hf} > 0$, with $H_{hmhm} < 0$ and $H_{hfhf} < 0$ and $H_{hmhf} < 0$ for the second derivatives. This last assumption means that the contributions h_m and h_f to household work H are substitutes. To avoid corner solutions suppose that $V'(0) = G'(0) = \infty$, $V'(T) = G'(T) = 0$ and

$$\lim_{h_m \to 0} \left(\frac{H_{h_m}}{H_{h_f}} \right) = \lim_{h_f \to 0} \left(\frac{H_{h_f}}{H_{h_m}} \right) = \infty .$$

6.3 The Stackelberg game

Utility maximization yields the following Nash equilibrium condition in which the spouses move simultaneously:

$$\text{(6.1)} \qquad \frac{V'(l_f)}{V'(l_m)} = \frac{w_f G'}{w_m G'} = \frac{w_f}{w_m} = \frac{H_{h_f}}{H_{h_m}}$$

[62] We will use capital letters to denote the aggregate level of the public good and small letters for the spouses' contributions to those public goods. An index used with capital letters will denote, as usual in the literature, the first (partial) derivative. When used with a small letter, the index will denote the origin of the contribution, *male* and *female*.

For equal wage rates of husband and wife, the same amounts of leisure time result. This is in clear contrast to empirical observation. The simultaneous Nash model does not provide an adequate explanation for the gender specific leisure gap.

What if husband and wife do not decide on their time use simultaneously? In light of men's continued status advantages in the economic domain, women are socialized to adapt their work hours around the needs of their families. In a study of "investments of time" by men and women in the U.S., Thomas Juster (1985b) found men to have more control over their time than women. He attributed this to a social structure where male roles are more purposive and female roles are more residually determined. Since in most households, women's wage income is still viewed as the second income, it seems plausible to assume that men "dominate" the family decision process on time allocation by deciding first. In economic terms, this means that the husband is the Stackelberg leader and maximizes his utility for a given choice of his wife.

The wages w_m and w_f are set exogenously. Both wages are certain and observable by all parties. The time structure of the game is the following:

1. The husband makes his choice about outside (money earning) work and housework.

2. The husband's choice is observed by his wife.

3. The wife chooses her optimal amount of work.

Since there is no uncertainty and the wife takes into account the decision of her spouse, we solve the problem backwards, calculating first the wife's optimal behavior as the Stackelberg follower. Her first order conditions are given by

$$\frac{\partial U^f(h_m, h_f, g_m, g_f)}{\partial g_f} = -V'(l_f) + w_f G' = 0 \tag{6.2}$$

$$\frac{\partial U^f(h_m, h_f, g_m, g_f)}{\partial h_f} = -V'(l_f) + H_{h_f} = 0, \tag{6.3}$$

where the indices denote the partial derivative with respect to the variables and the arguments are omitted for the sake of clarity. The budget constraint has been eliminated by setting $l_i = T_i - g_i - h_i$, $i=f,m$. These first order conditions implicitly define the wife's best response functions $g_f(g_m, h_m)$ *and* $h_f(g_m, h_m)$ for a given choice of her Stackelberg husband. By the implicit function theorem, it can be shown:

(6.4) $$\frac{\partial g_f(g_m,h_m)}{\partial g_m} = \frac{-w_f w_m G''(V'' + H_{h_f h_f})}{D} < 0$$

(6.5) $$\frac{\partial g_f(g_m,h_m)}{\partial h_m} = \frac{V'' H_{h_m h_f})}{D} > 0$$

(6.6) $$\frac{\partial h_f(g_m,h_m)}{\partial g_m} = \frac{w_f w_m G'' V''}{D} > 0$$

(6.7) $$\frac{\partial g_f(g_m,h_m)}{\partial h_m} = \frac{-(w_f{}^2 G'' + V'')H_{h_m h_f}}{D} < 0,$$

where the denominator is $D = V''- (w_f{}^2G'' + V'')(V'' + H_{hfhf})$. D equals the determinant of the 2x2 unbordered Hessian corresponding to the wife's optimization problem. It is therefore positive. That the reaction functions (6.4) and (6.7) are negative is a well known fact in the literature of private provision of public goods (see for instance Bergstrom et al. 1986). If the husband contributes more to one public good, the wife has an incentive to reduce her contribution to this public good, e.g. to do less out-of-home or homework, respectively. The reaction functions (6.5) and (6.6) are different. Consider equation (6.5): If the husband contributes more to housework $dh_m > 0$, this decreases the wife's marginal utility of household work, since we have assumed h_f and h_m to be substitutes. Therefore, the wife shifts time from house hold work into gainful employment and leisure. Equation (6.6) shows that the wife will react with an increased contribution to household production if the husband makes a higher contribution to the common income $dg_m > 0$.

We can formulate the maximization problem of the Stackelberg husband as

$$\max U^m(h_m,g_m) =$$
$$V(l_m) + G(w_m g_m + w_f g_f(g_m,h_m)) + H(h_m,h_f(g_m,h_m)),$$

which leads to the following first order conditions

(6.8) $$\frac{\partial U^m(h_m,h_f,g_m,g_f)}{\partial g_m} = -V'(l_m) + w_m G' + w_f G' \frac{\partial g_f}{\partial g_m} + H_{h_f} \frac{\partial h_f}{\partial g_m} = 0$$

$$\text{(6.9)}\quad \frac{\partial U^m(h_m,h_f,g_m,g_f)}{\partial h_m} = -V'(l_m) + w_f G' \frac{\partial g_f}{\partial h_m} + H_{h_m} + H_{h_f}\frac{\partial h_f}{\partial h_m} = 0 .$$

Combining the four first order conditions (6.2), (6.3), (6.8) and (6.9) we obtain the following optimality conditions for the time allocation of the couple:

$$\text{(6.10)}\quad \frac{V'(l_f)}{V'(l_m)} = \frac{w_f G'}{w_m G' + w_f G' \frac{\partial g_f}{\partial g_m} + H_{h_f}\frac{\partial h_f}{\partial g_m}}$$

$$\text{(6.11)}\quad = \frac{H_{h_f}}{H_{h_m} + w_f G' \frac{\partial g_f}{\partial h_m} + H_{h_f}\frac{\partial h_f}{\partial h_m}}$$

If we set the reaction functions equal to zero, we arrive at the non-cooperative simulataneous Nash solution (6.1) from above.

In the following, let us concentrate on interior equilibria. These are the cases where the wife doing paid market work has a "double burden" because she also contributes most of homework, resulting in less leisure time for her than for her husband. From the wife's first-order conditions (6.2) and (6.3) we obtain $H_{hf} = wG'$. The right hand side (RHS) of equation (6.10) simplifies to:

$$w_m G' + w_f G' \frac{\partial g_f}{\partial g_m} + H_{h_f}\frac{\partial h_f}{\partial g_m} = w_m G' + w_f G'\left(\frac{\partial g_f}{\partial g_m} + \frac{\partial h_f}{\partial g_m}\right)$$

$$= \frac{w_m}{w_f} + \left(\frac{\partial g_f}{\partial g_m} + \frac{\partial h_f}{\partial g_m}\right).$$

In an analogous way, we transform the RHS of condition (6.11) and arrive at the following equilibrium conditions:

$$\text{(6.12)}\quad \frac{V'(l_f)}{V'(l_m)} = \frac{1}{\frac{w_m}{w_f} + \frac{\partial g_f}{\partial g_m} + \frac{\partial h_f}{\partial g_m}} = \frac{1}{\frac{H_{h_m}}{H_{h_f}} + \frac{\partial g_f}{\partial h_m} + \frac{\partial h_f}{\partial h_m}}$$

Consider now the special case where the market wages of both partners are equal, $w_m = w_f$. Even when both have identical contribution costs to the public goods, we would expect the husband to exploit his Stackelberg advantage. Consequently, he reduces his contributions to the public goods and is able to enjoy more leisure, compared to the simultaneous-move Nash equilibrium. If both wages are equal, the husband benefits from his Stackelberg advantage in the following way:

(6.13) $$l_f < l_m$$

(6.14) $$V'(l_f) > V'(l_m)$$

(6.15) $$1 > \underbrace{\frac{w_m}{w_f}}_{=1} + \underbrace{\left(\frac{\partial g_f}{\partial g_m} + \frac{\partial h_f}{\partial g_m}\right)}_{<0},$$

For equal wages condition (6.15) is always fulfilled. Intuitively, this is the case because

(6.16) $$\left|\frac{\partial g_f}{\partial g_m}\right| > \frac{\partial h_f}{\partial g_m},$$

that is, if the husband contributes more to the public good market work, $dg_m > 0$, this always leads to a greater (absolute) change of his wife's commitment to G than of her commitment to H. In other words, the "direct" effect (in absolute terms) exceeds the "indirect" effect.

Let's turn to more general cases. Suppose $w_m \geq w_f$ and let w_R be the wage ratio[63], $w_R := w_m/w_f$ If the wife earns a higher wage, the wage ratio is less than one. Due to condition (6.15), the Stackelberg model makes a strong prediction. Since the wage ratio is smaller than one and the second term is always negative, the right side of the inequality (6.15) is smaller than one: the condition will always be fulfilled as long as the husband earns a lower wage. Thus, women outearning their husbands indeed enjoy less leisure than their partners. A negative wage gap always leads to a positive leisure gap. The model thus provides an economic explanation for the findings of Brines (1994) and Daly (1996) concerning couples where the wives earn higher wages and still enjoy less leisure time than their partners.

---

[63] While the wage gap is usually understood as a *difference* in wages of men and women, $\Delta w = w_m - w_f$, it will be more useful to consider the wage *ratio* in relative terms her.

As the male relative wage increases, the wife's leisure disadvantage diminishes and the husband's leisure time decreases. For equal wages $w_m = w_f$, the condition is fulfilled independent of the wage level and the specific functional form of the utility function. The husband is able to extract a leisure rent from his Stackelberg leadership, even though both spouses have the same market productivity.

As the male wage increases, the wage ratio in the RHS of (6.15) increases too. Without making further assumptions, it is not possible to say that the RHS of (6.15) increases monotonically in the wage ratio, because of the income effect associated with a wage change. The assumption that for a sufficiently high wage the husband reduces his work time (that is, the income effect compensates the negative substitution effect) does not guarantee monotonicity. Therefore the structure is still too general.

But for a very high pay differential the direct effect of the wage gap is higher than the reaction effects, i.e. the RHS of (6.15) is greater than one. In this situation the husband enjoys less leisure than his spouse *despite* being the Stackelberg leader. Intuitively, this happens because his market productivity is so much higher than his wife's that it dilutes his Stackelberg advantage. We know about the reaction functions of the RHS of (6.15) that, in absolute terms, the direct effect on g_f of a change in g_m exceeds the indirect effect of h_f (see inequality (6.16)). Since even the direct effect can never be greater than 1, we obtain

$$0 < \frac{\partial h_f}{\partial g_m} < \left|\frac{\partial g_f}{\partial g_m}\right| < 1. \tag{6.17}$$

The bracketed term in inequality (6.15) is always negative, but never smaller than -1. For a wage ratio greater than 2, the RHS of (6.15) will always be bigger than 1:

$$\frac{w_m}{w_f} + \left(\frac{\partial g_f}{\partial g_m} + \frac{\partial h_f}{\partial g_m}\right) > 2 + \underbrace{\left(\frac{\partial g_f}{\partial g_m} + \frac{\partial h_f}{\partial g_m}\right)}_{-1<(.)<0} > 1 \tag{6.18}$$

$$V'(l_m) > V'(l_f) \tag{6.19}$$

$$l_m < l_f \tag{6.20}$$

To summarize, we expect a negative non-monotonic relationship between the wage gap and the leisure gap. When the husband earns less than his wife he should enjoy more leisure than his wife. The husbands wins from both his Stackelberg leadership and his wife's higher productivity in the marketplace. As the wage gap diminishes and turns positive, the husband's increased market productivity makes him shift some time from leisure to market work. His wife reacts by reducing her commitment to market work and increasing both household work and leisure time. For a large enough wage gap, the leisure gap turns negative and the husband enjoys less free time than his wife.

6.4 Conclusions

In this Chapter leisure time decisions of a couple are explicitly modelled. This allows us to establish a direct link between the leisure gap and the wage gap between spouses. Within a Stackelberg setting it can also be shown that even with equal wage rates men enjoy more leisure than their wives but with larger wage differentials, this leisure gap will diminish and eventually turn negative.

Although wages are not explicitly modeled, this approach helps to explain the persisting leisure and wage inequality observed between women and men. Social structures that favor the man to make the first move lead to an intra-family time allocation that keeps women out of full-time employment, because that maximizes their disposable free time or minimizes their leisure reduction, respectively. As long as part-time jobs are paid less (on an hourly base) than full-time occupations and are associated with poorer promotion prospects the result is a persisting wage gap between the sexes.

The model shows that gender inequality within the household cannot be abolished by "simply" closing the wage gap between male and female employees, since even (or particularly) with a wage differential of zero, men dispose of more leisure. This result is due to the Stackelberg husband's advantage in deciding first on his provision of the family public goods. Hence, if the policy goal is to abolish gender inequality, one also has to change social structures that define gender roles and that are decisive for any asymmetries in family decision making.

It must be noted that all results are derived within a static setting. In a dynamic context employment might also bear human capital effects that have private good character and that are missed in this static model (see Chapter 4).

To conclude, in this model of private provision of family public goods the leisure gap and the wage gap form a stable equilibrium of gender inequality. The gender-specific leisure gap has been shown to result from the pay differential between women and men as well as from gender inequality that is determined by social structures. These structures are not fixed, but could be subject to change, though.

7 The leisure gap between working parents

7.1 Introduction

Women, especially working mothers, have less leisure time on average than men. This is a well-known fact confirmed by nearly every survey on individual time use[64]. In the German Time Budget Survey of 1991/92 the overall "leisure gap" between the sexes amounts to more than 20 minutes on an average day (Statistisches Bundesamt 1995). When it comes to working adults the gender-specific difference increases to over half an hour for those employed full-time. The greatest leisure gap, however, can be observed in households where both husband and wife hold full-time employment and where there are small children to be cared for. For these couples male partners dispose of one hour more per day than their spouses. Expressed more dramatically, this translates to over nine 40-hours "leisure weeks" per year (two and a half more months of vacation) for fathers with working wives.

While this work- and child-related pattern of the leisure gap is hardly unique to Germany, the size of this gap differs substantially across countries. Whereas in the U.S. the gender-specific leisure differential for employed spouses averages 2.3 hours per week (in 1985), the 1995-Russian gap amounts to four additional weekly hours for men (Robinson/Godbey 1997). According to ILO statistics the average male West-European works a combined 43 hours per week at home and on the job, while the female West-European's weekly work load sums up to 48 hours. In Italy for instance, women work 28% more hours than men, in Austria 12% more, and in France 11% more, as the 1995 *Human Development Report* (United Nations 1995) found in its review of time use studies.

---

[64] E.g. see Juster (1985a), Shelton (1992), Ehling (1996), Robinson/Godbey (1997), Statistisches Bundesamt (1998a).

While most time use studies investigate how men and women allocate their time to paid and unpaid work in great detail, there have been few contributions to address an extremely important question regarding the division of time by gender: why is it that women have even less leisure time relative to men, the more hours they work for pay and the more children they have? This is the question to be considered in this chapter. Drawing on economic theories of time use as well as on the bargaining literature a simple model of the intrafamily distribution of leisure will be discussed and tested empirically.

One of those rare contributions that actually provide structural explanations is by Rosemary Deem (1982) who hypothesizes women's deeper commitment to the familial ideology as one possible explanation for women's lower participation in out-of-home leisure and sport activities[65]. Women and men might have distinctive experiences of time because of the different demands that are placed on them and the degree of control that they have over their own allocation of time (Daly 1996). Women are socialized according to an ethic of care associated with a diminished sense of entitlement to free time for themselves. Joan Huber's and Glenna Spitze's argument (1983) points to a cultural determination of families' time use arrangements. According to their study it is the size of the wife's wage income that influences intrafamily time allocation and, thus, the husband's and wife's respective leisure times. Proceeding from Huber and Spitze the sociologist Arlie Hochschild (1989) argues that there is more to the leisure gap between wives and husbands than men's higher wages. In her seminal work on *The second shift* she concludes that this gap also reflects an interplay of gender strategies: Women who out-earn their husbands make up for doing too well at work by doing more at home, following the "principle of balancing" (Hochschild 1989: 278). As a result we observe full-time working women actually ending up with relatively less free time.

For these sociological interpretations one wonders whether there exists a complementary economic explanation for the persistent leisure gap. Existing economic theories of intrafamily time allocation do not provide a conclusive answer to this question. On the one hand, there is the traditional framework of joint utility maximization within the household (e.g. Becker 1965 and Gronau 1973, 1977). Whereas Becker did not distinguish between housework and leisure - and thus merely came to the conclusion (known as the specialization argument) that women spend less time working for pay and more time at home if their wages are lower than their partners' wages - Gronau introduced the distinction between three time uses: market labor, household labor and leisure. Given a wage differential between men and women the Gronau model also predicts a female specialization in household production and a male specialization in market work. However, for the case of complete spe-

[65] In her own leisure study she finds little confirmation, though.

cialization what cannot be derived, is the amount of leisure time for each partner.

Bargaining models or private-provision-of-public-goods models, on the other hand, try to explain a couples' time allocation by means of the respective "bargaining power" of each spouse[66]. In contrast to the traditional theory these approaches explicitly account for the distributive aspects of intrafamily time use and in this respect they provide an appropriate framework for explaining the gender-related division of time.

In the present chapter[67] a bargaining model is proposed where the individual amount of leisure time is treated as the outcome of an alternating offers game between family members over the distribution of leisure time, with leisure being the only private consumption good in the household. Hence, observed leisure time is interpreted as the outcome of a time use arrangement between partners that has been contracted at the family formation stage (when the decision for having children has been made) and that will be temporarily static during the early family phase (when small children have to be taken care of). Due to the female "biological clock" or due to socially determined gender roles that assign women responsibility for family matters, a woman might have a higher rate of time preference to enter the early family phase, i.e. to have children, than her partner. This impatience results in a lower bargaining position relative to that of her husband. In the decision-making process she will thus end up with relatively less free time at her disposal.

Following a presentation of descriptive statistics for the division of leisure in German families, the structure of the model will be outlined in the third section. Using data from the German Time Budget Survey of 1991/92 the relative bargaining power of women measured by their share of leisure time in the household will be estimated. The paper concludes with a discussion of the main empirical findings.

7.2 Basic facts of intrafamily distribution of leisure

The German Time Budget Survey was conducted from fall 1991 through summer 1992. In 7200 households all members above the age of 11 years filled out time diaries for two subsequent days. The resulting 32,000 diaries provide time-use information in five-minute intervals. When participating in multiple activities the respondents identified what they considered their primary and secondary activities but only primary activities are analyzed in this

[66] For comprehensive surveys on bargaining models of family decision making see e.g. Bergstrom (1996) and Lundberg/Pollak (1996). Lommerud (1997) discusses noncooperative private-provision-of-public-goods games.

[67] This chapter is a revised and extended version of Beblo (1999).

study. All activities that had been described in these diaries were then standardized according to a catalogue comprising 200 activities, among these more than 20 different leisure activities[68].

Following the definition given in Chapter 6, leisure or private time is defined as time spent on self-determined activities. Since these activities are pursued for their own sake, for the benefit of the individual performing them, these activities cannot be delegated to anyone else and then be transferred back. This concept of leisure is called the *third person criterion* (see Schäfer/Schwarz 1996 and Ott 1999). Whereas labor refers to all activities that are inputs of a production process the output of which is interpersonally transferable, leisure does not yield any such outputs that could be traded in return for other services. Sport activities, watching TV or eating and sleeping for instance, by this definition, are all considered leisure activities.

In modern economic theories of time allocation three major time uses are generally modeled: time devoted to (paid) labor, time devoted to (unpaid) labor at home and leisure time. Hardly any attention is paid to physiological regeneration such as sleeping, eating and other personal needs activities. Regardless of the extensive literature on the economics of sleeping (see e.g. Biddle/Hamermesh 1990) these activities are essentially taken as exogenously given and fixed for each individual. Nonetheless this ignores the fact that women, in particular single-parent mothers, often cut back their sleep hours, economizing regeneration time, in order to cope with the double burden of working for a living and looking after their children (Strober/Weinberg 1980). For this reason two different concepts of leisure will be used what follows. First, leisure will be considered in a narrower sense, including only those activities that are commonly regarded as leisure activities or hobbies. A broader concept of leisure, denoted as private time, also includes physiological regeneration (sleeping, eating and personal care) as part of the exclusively private consumption time. Both concepts are considered in an overview of the average daily time use (including weekdays and Sundays) of 18 to 50-year old couples in the Time Budget Survey, listed in Table 7.1.

For men and for women leisure and private time both decrease with their attachment to the labor market and the household. Men with full-time employment spend a greater share of their day working (paid and unpaid work) and, accordingly, enjoy significantly less leisure than part-timers or nonemployed. The same pattern is true for women, even though their regeneration generally takes up slightly more time than men's, whereas their amount of pure leisure time is lower.

---

[68] For a detailed description of the data set see Statistisches Bundesamt (1995) and Blanke et al. (1996).

Table 7.1: The average time use of couples age 18-50

	Men			Women		
	not empl.	part-time	full-time	not empl.	part-time	full-time
			Hours per day			
No children						
Total working time	4.35	5.42	9.40	5.87	7.60	9.55
Unpaid work	3.90	2.45	2.42	5.40	4.32	3.17
Paid work	0.45	2.97	6.85	0.47	3.28	6.38
Private time	17.63	16.83	14.57	17.37	15.83	14.27
Physiolog. regeneration	11.02	11.27	10.00	11.90	10.80	10.27
Leisure	6.62	5.57	4.57	5.47	5.05	4.00
Children <6 years						
Total working time	5.67	8.82	9.90	8.98	9.43	10.48
Unpaid work	5.38	3.90	3.20	8.85	6.63	5.20
Paid work	0.30	4.92	6.70	0.13	2.80	5.28
Private time	16.87	14.87	13.90	14.70	13.43	13.20
Physiolog. regeneration	10.97	9.98	9.87	10.48	10.28	10.08
Leisure	5.90	4.88	4.03	4.22	4.15	3.12
Children 6-12 years						
Total working time	6.45	8.05	9.42	7.92	8.87	10.33
Unpaid work	5.45	2.72	2.77	7.75	5.95	4.27
Paid work	1.00	5.33	6.65	0.17	2.92	5.92
Private time	17.12	15.63	14.47	15.75	14.92	13.65
Physiolog. regeneration	11.75	9.95	10.10	10.77	10.55	10.15
Leisure	5.37	5.68	4.37	4.97	4.37	3.50
n	129	51	1708	723	318	721

Data source: Author's calculations based on the German Time Budget Survey 1991/92.
Note: The minutes missing to the total of 24 hours are due to non-assignable time uses such as preparation time. Different numbers of men and women are due to item/unit non-response of the partner.

Children living in the household reduce time used for physiological regeneration as well as leisure time for both parents. The effect on female time use, however, is much larger. As soon as a child under 6 years is present non-employed women's leisure falls from 5.5 to 4.2 hours and that of full-time employed women decreases from 4 to 3.1 hours[69]. Men holding a full-time employment, on the contrary, only face a reduction in free time by slightly more than half an hour (from 4.6 to 4 hours). Accordingly the gender-specific leisure gap is at its maximum of nearly one hour for full-time working mothers and fathers with (at least) one pre-school child.[70]

These averages show that in general individual leisure time depends on the amount of time allocated to other uses (paid work as well as unpaid work). It is also related to the individual shadow price of time according e.g. to the number and the ages of children in the household, since leisure time falls with small children being present. Thus far, our observations conform with the predictions of the standard time allocation theory[71]. No conclusive answer has yet been given as to the difference in male and female leisure time, though.

7.3 The distribution of leisure as an alternating offers game

In order to develop an economic explanation of the leisure gap a bargaining model is now proposed where the individual amount of leisure time is considered the outcome of an alternating offers game between family members.

7.3.1 The setting

In the following we shall consider the case of a household/family with two interacting individuals. Generally, these individuals could be brother and sister, parent and child or a pair of friends. To illustrate the leisure gap quantified in the previous section and to match the specific setting, the analysis will be restricted to the husband-and-wife constellation, with the terms husband and wife being defined in a technical way to include also cohabiting couples. Each individual has to make his or her own time allocation and consumption decisions. These individual choices, however, are interrelated with

---

[69] Note that this greater drop in female "gross" leisure time is also accompanied by a higher amount of women's time that is reported to be leisure but that is at the same time devoted to productive side activities such as having an eye on the children. For German parents of pre-school children this "pseudo leisure" only takes up 6% of the father's, but 13% of the mother's free time. The gendered division of primary and secondary activities within the household has been investigated in more detail by Holz (1998). Using U.S. data Shaw (1992) also found that mothers' leisure involves more work components than fathers'.

[70] This one-hour gap is partly offset by the greater amount of time that even full-time employed women devote to their personal care. The resulting difference in private time, however, still accounts for 42 minutes per day less for women. With children between 6 and 12 years of age present it is as high as 49 minutes.

[71] See Becker (1965) and Gronau (1973, 1977).

the partner's decision problem through the provision and sharing of family public goods. Time can be allocated among three principal uses: paid work, unpaid work and leisure. Time spent in paid labor yields wage income that is regarded as a family public good since housing, transportation or, generally, the family's living standard is purchased with that income. Time spent in unpaid labor also yields a public good to the family. Household production such as child care, a clean house and a nice yard only have to be provided by some family member for all the others to benefit from. The only private good in this model is the individual amount of leisure time. Intrahousehold bargaining over the distribution of household resources therefore implies bargaining over individual time allocation, namely time that can be disposed of freely by each partner. In this context, a good bargain really means getting away with more leisure time which is the only good that can be consumed individually. Housing, child care etc., on the contrary, are consumed publicly. It is assumed that they are not associated with distributive conflicts between the partners. As a consequence, within such a setting it is solely the amount of leisure time that has to be referred to when analyzing outcomes of intrafamily bargaining. The relative bargaining power of the spouses should be reflected in the hours each of them is able to devote to individual leisure activities.

Two qualifications must be mentioned immediately. First, to keep the analysis simple we must ignore any dual-use leisure activity associated with other time uses. A coffee break at work for instance, or a training course could easily be simultaneously leisure and hours devoted to paid market work. Also with regard to the time use "unpaid work" activities such as arts and crafts or playing with children are certainly not only characterized by productive but also consumptive aspects. In fact there exists hardly any activity where a sharp distinction between leisure and work can be made, instead many activities yield the joint products (paid or unpaid) work and play[72]. In the empirical study this qualification is partly addressed by analyzing what the respondents themselves identified as their primary activity. That is, they subjectively reported whether they considered their time use to be leisure or work. Second, the model abstracts from any private goods other than the partners' leisure hours. In other words, even clothing is considered a public good to the family. Although the differentiation used in this paper is a very restrictive one, it has the advantage of being compatible with empirical investigation,

---

[72] Shaw (1992) demonstrated that particularly family leisure is experienced differently by fathers and mothers and that women are more likely to report family time with children as an experience of mixed leisure and work.

given the data available. Due to data constraints the model has to be specified with leisure as the only private good[73].

If we now take a closer look at a conceivable specification of a static bargaining setting as it is described above, the alternating offers game developed by Ariel Rubinstein (1982) and extended by Kenneth Binmore (1987) appears to provide an appropriate framework[74].

7.3.2 The structure of the game

In the Rubinstein alternating offers game the decision making process of the couple will have the following structure: At the family formation stage - i.e. when the couple is deciding whether or not to have a child - the players (husband and wife) make a series of alternating offers to each other as how to distribute utility between themselves. Since utility is completely measured in terms of individual leisure time, they bargain over their respective shares of the household's total leisure that will be fixed for the early family phase (L_f and L_m, where $L_f + L_m = 1$)[75]. Once an offer has been made by one partner, the other one must either accept or reject the offer before making a counter offer. Due to impatience each individual i discounts future utility by a delay or discount factor $\delta_i<1$, so that the utility to spouse i of receiving L_i units of leisure in period t is $L_i\delta_i^t$. The bargain is settled, or, in other words, the division of free time is decided, as soon as some offer has been accepted. This game is characterized by an infinite bargaining horizon, complete information for both partners and delay costs associated with postponing the agreement.

---

[73] There does not exist any public use file, at least not in Germany, with information on individual consumption of goods and services as well as time use and the individuals' and households' socio-demographic background variables. The German Time Budget Survey used, for instance, does not include any expenditure data.

[74] This framework is typically applied to bargaining contests on sales contracts. Another application is presented by Shaked/Sutton (1984) who derive involuntary unemployment as a perfect equilibrium of a bargaining model with asymmetry between "insiders" and "outsiders". Bergstrom (1997) discusses the alternating-offers game in the context of family economics. He considers a married couple where the spouses make offers and counteroffers on a general utility distribution or ask for divorce as an outside option.

[75] The total amount of leisure time to be divided is set equal to unity for once and for all. This is a strong restriction since in real life the sum of female and male leisure hours is determined endogenously within the family decision making process over time allocation. One could indeed imagine a two-stage determination of intrafamily time use where in the first stage the partners choose the total amount of family public goods they want to consume. Secondly they bargain on who is going to provide the required time input to produce these goods and who receives which share of the resulting family leisure time.

As the time between proposals becomes smaller, in the limit the alternating offers game has a unique subgame perfect equilibrium in which the pie is to be divided in the first period with *i*'s (e.g. the female's) share being $\phi = \dfrac{\log \delta_i}{\log \delta_f + \log \delta_m}$ and *i=f, m* (Binmore 1987). Hence, one partner gets the fraction ϕ of total leisure time and the other one gets $1-\phi$. That is, the more impatient partner gets a smaller and the less impatient gets a bigger slice of the pie.

Figure 7.1: Asymmetric Nash bargaining solution

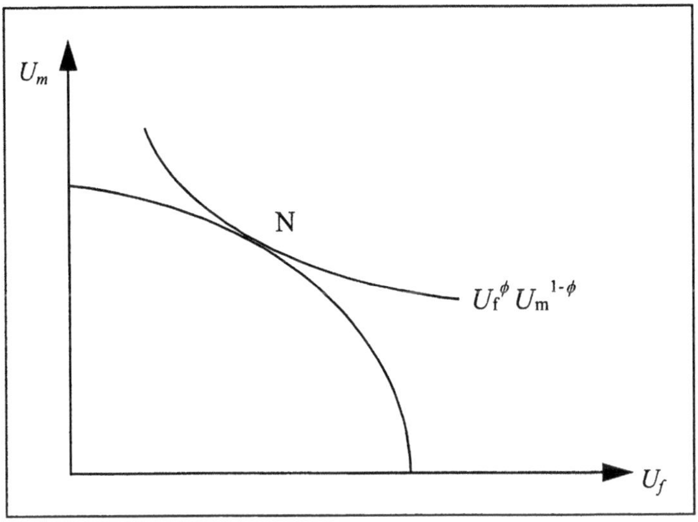

As Binmore (1987) pointed out, the perfect equilibrium outcome to this alternating offers game is an approximation to the generalized Nash bargaining solution to:

$$\max N = U_f(L_f)^{\phi} \cdot U_m(L_m)^{1-\phi},$$

where U_f denotes the utility of the wife, depending solely on her amount of leisure time, and U_m denotes the utility of the male, also determined by his own leisure hours, with the bargaining weights ϕ and $1-\phi$ as functions of the players' discount factors. The asymmetric Nash bargaining solution is demonstrated graphically in Figure 7.1.

The slope of the bargaining frontier is represented by $\frac{\phi}{1-\phi}$, indicating the marginal rate of utility transfer between wife and husband. Since utility is measured exclusively in terms of leisure time, the tangency point N of the Nash maximization curve with the convex bargaining set is identified by the combination of respective leisure hours L_f and L_m, i.e. the contracted time use arrangement between the spouses. The wife's share of leisure time $\frac{L_f}{L_f + L_m}$ can therefore be interpreted as a measure of her relative bargaining power. That is, the higher the wife's relative bargaining power the greater her share of leisure time will be if this is regarded the only private good to be consumed within the household.

The intrafamily leisure contract that is being bargained over crucially depends on the partners' discount rates. In case the two partners have equal discount rates the resulting utility distribution would be the same as in the symmetric Nash bargaining solution. With identical utility functions husband and wife would thus receive equal amounts of leisure. However, as illustrated in the preceding section this is not observed for actual time allocation choices, especially not for working couples with small children. One plausible explanation for the observed leisure gap between men and women could be a gender-specific rate of time preference that determines the intrahousehold distribution of disposable time in favor of men. Such a gender-specific rate of time preference could be due to the female "biological clock" and social norms regarding women's responsibility for managing jobs and kids. As is the message of much of the sociological literature: "Giving birth accentuates and dramatizes the difference between male and female conceptualizations of time. [...] Gendered time perceptions change according to the different demands that are associated with social roles for men and women." (Daly 1996: 145-146). A woman who wants to have a child faces a relatively inflexible time horizon to realize her plans - for obvious biological reasons - and hence, has a relatively high time preference rate as a function of her actual age. For a man, on the contrary, there is no need to hurry since his time horizon is much larger than his (current) spouse's. In other words he displays greater patience with regard to family formation. Accordingly, his time preference rate is lower[76]. These gender-specific rates of time preference together with socially determined gender roles assigning family care a woman's key responsibility result in different discount rates and, thus, asymmetric bar-

[76] Unless of course he has a special preference for his current spouse to be the mother of his children. But with regard to an increasing divorce rate and an even higher separation rate for cohabiting couples, this is expected to affect the average male time preference rate only marginally.

gaining weights for men and women in the Nash maximization problem. The observed leisure gap is then due to women and men's different experience of time that can be attributed to biological as well as social factors.

In the following we may interpret a household's actual time use arrangement as the result of a sharing-rule on private good consumption in the household, using Chiappori's terminology (1988, 1997). Since leisure is the only private good in this setting, the sharing-rule tells us the proportion of total free time each individual can dispose of given her own and her partner's respective discount factors that are themselves determined by bargaining variables. The contracted sharing-rule is assumed to be effective for the early family period when small children need to be cared for. Hence, I am proposing a temporarily static model where intrafamily time allocation is neither bargained on a day-to-day basis nor is it fixed once and for all from marriage to household dissolution. Instead, time use arrangements are re-bargained rather infrequently whenever major changes in household characteristics take place, such as the birth of the first child or the time when older children do not require continual care anymore. Once an arrangement has been settled it will be effective for a number of years (until the next change takes place). There are no investment effects associated with time spent in gainful employment.

In the next section we examine couples' actual sharing rules, i.e. their realized leisure distribution during the early family phase and treat them as the outcomes of time use arrangements that have been contracted just before family formation. This way the determinants of a couples' sharing rule can be analyzed empirically.

7.4 The distribution of leisure – estimation results

Using data from the German Time Budget Survey on working couples (married as well as cohabiting) between the age of 18-50 the following linear representation of the sharing rule ϕ will be estimated, with ϕ measuring the wife's share of family leisure time and ε being the mean zero normally distributed random error term that represents the effects of any omitted variables:

$$\begin{aligned}\phi = \phi_0 &+ \phi_1 \cdot \text{biological clock}\\ &+ \phi_2 \cdot \text{biological clock squared}\\ &+ \phi_3 \cdot \text{female wage}\\ &+ \phi_4 \cdot \text{male wage}\\ &+ \phi_5 \cdot \text{female-male wage ratio}\\ &+ \phi_6 \cdot \text{dummy pre-school child}\\ &+ \phi_7 \cdot \text{dummy child of age 6-12}\end{aligned}$$

$$+ \ \phi_8 \cdot \text{tenure of partnership}$$
$$+ \ \phi_9 \cdot \text{total household income}$$
$$+ \ \varepsilon.$$

In order to allow for gender-specific rates of time preference, an indicator variable for the "biological clock" has been included in the regression. The bio clock variable counts a woman's years of age above age 30 when a small child (up to age 5) is living in the household. To illustrate, a 37-year old mother of at least one pre-school child is assigned the value 7 (7 over 30) compared to a woman of 32 with a pre-school child who is assigned a value of 2 and a woman with no pre-school who is assigned a value of 0. This variable does not only tell us whether a time use arrangement has already been contracted within the household at all, but also *when* this arrangement was settled. The higher the value of this biological indicator, the older the woman was at the time of contracting. The 37-year old mother has faced a shorter time horizon than did the woman of 32 e.g. when bargaining over future leisure distribution had taken place. As a consequence we expect the older mother to have been willing to make more concessions regarding her share of family leisure time.[77] In general one would expect time use arrangements to be less favorable the higher the mother's age, i.e. less time on her bio clock. Since couples without pre-school children are not considered to have reached the early family phase or still be in that stage of the life cycle, for them we do not observe such family-formation time use arrangements. And so, the biological indicator has been set to 0.

The bargaining argument implies a negative correlation between the bio clock and the female leisure share within a household. To allow for non-linear age-leisure patterns both a linear and a quadratic indicator term have been included in the regression equation. In the static setting of traditional time allocation theory, these variables would not be expected to show any effect at all, since all distribution rules had long been fixed in the marriage market prior to household formation and time use arrangements are not subject to re-bargaining within the family.

In addition to the wife's rate of time preference as reflected in the time on her biological clock, the wife's and husband's wages (their respective individual

[77] This can be viewed as a moderate and more continuous modeling of a couples' decision problem at the family formation stage than the prisoner's dilemma approach to fertility by Ott (1992). In Ott the non-cooperative Nash equilibrium always results in a decision against children, whereas here cooperation (i.e. having children) is feasible with the woman's leisure share reflecting her relative bargaining position.

income potentials[78]) are controlled for as additional determinants of their bargaining weights. A higher income potential implies greater bargaining power due to the improved outside option relative to the family contract. Consequently, the bargaining argument derived from the alternating offers game above would be consistent with a higher female wage being associated with more female leisure because of an improved bargaining position (similarly a higher male wage leading to less female leisure). The relative human capital measures, on the other hand, are only expected to matter in the bargaining case. Whereas, from a bargaining perspective, large disparities in individual income potentials are seen to have an impact on the spouses' relative bargaining positions and so their leisure shares, the specialization argument (derived from the traditional time allocation approach) does not predict any correlation between the wage ratio and time use decisions. It must be noted that it is not evident that the individual net income measure will show any effect on the distribution of leisure for married couples. Even if bargaining within the family takes place, married spouses' net wages might not be the appropriate measures of their bargaining weights due to tax treatment of the family as a single unit. Therefore it appears reasonable to use data on both married and unmarried couples to investigate the impact of policy measures specifically targeted at married couples.

To be able to interpret male and female leisure shares as indicators of the actual output distribution within households, only interior solutions to the time allocation problem are considered: only couples where both spouses are employed have been included in the sample. The sample is further restricted to respondents with a minimum of one minute devoted to the remaining two time uses housework and leisure in order to exclude any cases of rationing in time use. The final sample consists of a total of 1192 couples, 1018 of whom are married and 174 are unmarried.

Separate Ordinary Least Squares (OLS) regressions on the wife's share of leisure time have been run, one for married couples and one for cohabiting couples (see Table 7.2). The latter serve as a control group in order to identify marriage-specific behavior as e.g. induced by the tax-transfer system or other policy measures.

---

[78] Since pure labor income is not listed in the Time Budget Survey, total individual net income, reported for the preceding month, has been divided by actual working hours (in employment) to obtain a rough measure of the present wage or income potential of each partner. In a sensitivity analysis the impact of education (the only human capital variable available, since no information on work histories is provided) has been checked. No statistically significant effect was found, while all remaining results were substantially unchanged.

Table 7.2: OLS-regression of the female share of a household's total leisure time

	Female leisure share			
	Married couples		Cohabiting couples	
	Coefficient estimate	T-value	Coefficient estimate	T-value
Constant	.4737	24.30	.4845	18.69
Bio clock	.0079	1.20	.0990	2.33
Bio clock squared	-.0010	-1.61	-.0108	-1.79
Female wage	.0019	2.52	.0053	2.91
Male wage	.0010	1.61	-.0033	-2.99
Female-male wage ratio	.1167	1.00	-.0387	-1.94
Dummy child <6	-.0112	-.83	-.0716	-2.95
Dummy child 6-12	-.0084	-.84	.0366	1.44
Tenure of partnership	-.0000	-.03	-.0053	-2.75
Total household income	-.005	-1.91	.0058	.91
Adjusted R^2	.02		.20	

Data source: Author's calculations based on the German Time Budget Survey 1991/92.

Overall the regression equation provides a much better fit to the sample of cohabiting couples, where 20% of the variance in gender-specific leisure shares can be explained by the proposed age and income variables, than to the married sample (fraction of explained variance = 2%). Moreover, among cohabitors there is a stronger indication of bargaining on time use arrangements actually taking place within the household.[79]

With regard to the indicator variable "bio clock" the estimation results support the bargaining argument of the proposed alternating offers game. Again, in a static specialization model this variable would play no role. But since for the cohabiting couples the linear and the quadratic term of the indicator variable are jointly significant, the female leisure share seems to be inversely U-shaped with respect to the biological clock. The peak at age 35 means that above that age women face a drastic reduction in their share of leisure time if they have small children. According to the bargaining argument this might be

[79] With regard to the very restrictive definition of leisure, leisure-like activities within other time uses such as coffee breaks at work have been controlled for in sensitivity tests. The resulting pattern was substantively unchanged.

due to their higher rate of time preference ("bio clock") that results in a weaker bargaining position the older they are at the moment when the arrangement is contracted. This result holds even when controlling for the presence of small children through the inclusion of a dummy variable for preschool children (that is also inversely related to the sharing rule).

In previous time use studies the effect of age on available leisure time has been less clear (Juster 1985a, Firestone/Shelton 1994). In particular, no gender differences in the association between age and leisure time have been proposed. In a control estimation I could not find any relationship between age and the gender-specific leisure share either. Only with the inclusion of the interaction term "bio clock" that also controls for the couple's actual stage of the life cycle, i.e. especially the presence of children, was it possible to detect a dependence between the woman's age and her disposable free time.

Among cohabiting couples both wages, male and female, significantly correlate with the sharing rule in the way predicted by the bargaining model: The partial effects[80] show that the higher the wife's own income potential and the lower that of her partner, the higher will be her individual share of leisure. The coefficient estimates for the female-male wage ratio itself, on the other hand, reveal an inverse relation between the relative female contribution to the household and the sharing rule. In other words, the higher the woman's relative wage the less leisure she gets. The statistically significant negative sign (at the 10%-level) of the relative income measure does not support either setting, be it the traditional or the static Nash bargaining game proposed. It could be consistent with a sequential bargaining approach (as presented in Chapter 6) or a dynamic framework (shown in Chapter 4) where employment yields long-run effects due to human capital accumulation. As a result, highly educated women with high wages sacrifice leisure to supply labor because they expect this to raise their future income potential.

Whereas for married couples total household income has a negative impact on the female leisure share, cohabiting women's leisure is negatively related to the tenure of the relationship. Given that both tenure and leisure gap are smaller among cohabiting than among married couples, it appears that over the time of the relationship cohabitors' time allocation approaches that chosen by married couples - resulting in less leisure time for the female spouse.

The empirical evidence also suggests that while there is some indication for bargaining (in particular for the cohabiting couples), specialization according to comparative productivity advantages still plays an important role for intrafamily time allocation. Within the sample of married couples, bargaining effects are partly offset by specialization effects (see e.g. the positive coeffi-

[80] The partial effects are 0.048 for female wage and -0.0015 for male wage.

cient of the male wage). In addition, as mentioned earlier, the net wage of a married woman might not be an appropriate indicator of her human capital due to joint taxation. Since through tax splitting the first earner's wage is usually taxed at a lower rate whereas the additional earner's wage is hit by the spouse's high marginal tax rate, net income variables may be severely biased for married couples with differing incomes. For German tax and family policy with its main focus thus far not on the compatibility of job and family but rather on specialization by time or by person in one of the two areas, it is not surprising that such policy incentives have consequences. For this reason it would be interesting to analyze whether intrafamily time allocation in countries with different family policy, e.g. Sweden or Finland, and in particular their distribution of leisure, reveals stronger bargaining effects for married couples than does the German case.

7.5 Conclusions

Bargaining within families is so obvious as not to be a controversial point. This still leaves the timing and the frequency of bargaining to be explained. Is it more plausible that spouses already agree on a fixed sharing rule when they match on the marriage market, thereby anticipating all future income streams, or is family life accompanied by repeated bargaining about output, i.e. leisure, distribution? In the latter case the sharing rule would only be fixed for a given time use arrangement and would vary between different arrangements.

In this chapter an asymmetric Nash bargaining game was derived from an alternating offers game on the intrafamily distribution of leisure in which the partners' bargaining weights are functions of their discount factors or rates of time preference. A sharing rule for leisure was derived and statistically estimated using data from the German Time Budget Survey 1991/92. In the estimation partners' income potentials were controlled for as additional bargaining factors.

To summarize, the empirical results of this paper support the bargaining hypothesis of the proposed alternating offers game. The empirical evidence suggests that bargaining within the family takes place, since the distribution of leisure can be seen to vary with the gender-specific experience of time that is indicated by the woman's biological clock. Hence, the moment of family formation matters since this determines the female's rate of time preference and thus her bargaining power with respect to that of her partner when implicitly contracting time use arrangement. Second, the sharing rule not only depends on absolute wage levels but it is also the relative income potential that matters. In the simple static specialization model on the contrary, relative income would not be expected to have explanatory power.

One reason for the ambiguous results in the married sample could be the assumption that leisure is the sole private good in the household. Assuming labor income to be a pure family public good could indeed be too restrictive, if a reduction in leisure time were to be compensated by other private consumption goods. The distribution of leisure can only be interpreted as an indicator of a household's distribution of output or utility when all other private goods are equally distributed. This is not necessarily the case if leisure time can be compensated for or if it is given up in order to accumulate human capital, e.g. as would be predicted by the dynamic bargaining model of Ott (1992) that has been extended in Chapter 4. In this case, the leisure share alone cannot capture by itself a household's output distribution but only a portion of each member's private gain. In order to investigate this question in greater depth a richer data set, containing information on the distribution of all private goods, leisure as well as other consumption goods, would be required.

Another complicating factor can be found in German tax and family policy that is targeted to support the traditional breadwinner-cum-homemaker family and therefore promotes specialization within families. Even granting these qualifications, the bargaining approach implemented in this paper nevertheless provides an initial economic explanation for the gender-specific leisure gap observed between working parents. This explanation is also confirmed econometrically, and strongly so for cohabiting couples.

8 Resume

8.1 Principal findings

In the course of this dissertation different aspects of individual time use within a family context have been investigated. One theoretical study and three empirical applications of family bargaining models have been offered to explain particular time uses. The studies analyzed the distinct time uses employment, household production and leisure. The empirical analyses provide evidence that family time allocation is indeed determined by intra-household bargaining. These results are broadly consistent with and extend the existing empirical literature on family decision making. As noted throughout, intra-household decisions governing the division of work or the distribution of resources and welfare between family members are not merely characterized by a single bargaining rule. According to the social and cultural environment and according to the object of decision, one needs to consider cooperative and non cooperative elements or even common preferences of the family members.

The dynamic bargaining model of Chapter 4 treats labor force participation as having a strategic aspect with regard to future individual bargaining positions within the household. It predicts that with diminishing enforceability of the marriage contract women, and particularly women with small children, are less willing to give up market work in order to specialize in housework and child care. They have an incentive to stay in the labor market (at least on a part-time base) to protect themselves against the loss of bargaining power. This behavior could as well be interpreted as insurance against the risk of divorce. The empirical results for married women in the German Socio-economic Panel (GSOEP) reveal strong support for this hypothesis. The more unequal the couples' bargaining powers, the higher is the wife's incentive to improve her future bargaining position. The expected relative attractiveness of a woman's external alternative to marriage (the conflict payoff) with respect to that of her partner significantly determines her employment decision. As predicted by the dynamic bargaining model, the impact of the conflict payoff leads to higher labor force participation due to a lower reservation wage.

The empirical results of the panel-econometric estimation of the division of household work in Chapter 5 reveal that, allowing for variables identified by the traditional theory, gender-specific household activity is also influenced by the age difference between spouses. This difference serves as an indicator for a strategic advantage in family decision making in favor of the older spouse derived from a non-cooperative Stackelberg game. For married couples in the GSOEP the "home chores gap" between husband and wife is greater the larger their age difference.

In Chapters 6 and 7 the question has been addressed, how leisure is distributed among family members and why men are generally observed to enjoy more leisure time than women. In a private provision of family public goods model (Chapter 6) a direct link between the leisure gap and the wage gap between spouses is established. The model provides an economic explanation for the persistent inequality between women and men. Social structures that favor male dominance lead to an intra-family time allocation that keeps women out of full-time employment, because it allows them to maximize their disposable free time (minimizes their leisure reduction). As long as part-time jobs are paid less (on an hourly base) than full-time the result is a persistent average wage gap between the sexes.

Finally, a sharing rule for leisure time is theoretically derived and estimated using data from the German Time Budget Survey of 1991/92 (Chapter 7). Partners' bargaining weights are modeled as functions of their discount factors (rates of time preference). The empirical results reveal that the distribution of leisure varies with the gender-specific experience of time, here captured by the woman's biological clock. Hence, the moment of family formation matters since it determines the female's rate of time preference and thus her bargaining power with respect to that of her partner regarding time use arrangements. This finding is consistent with the bargaining hypothesis of the proposed alternating offers game. While the results for married couples do not unambiguously support the bargaining hypothesis, for cohabiting couples there is empirical evidence pointing to family bargaining over the individual share of leisure time.

8.2 Policy implications

The degree to which each of the assumptions imposed on household decision making reflects reality is an empirical issue but one that depends on the research or policy issue at hand. Clarity about the policy implications of the empirical findings presented is crucial inasmuch as the structure of decision making within the household may itself be subject to changing public policy. The competing models predict different effects of public transfers made to the household. These different impacts apply to the recipients of the transfers as well as to non-recipients since they depend on the way household members are interacting. Errors in understanding intrafamily decision making may thus result in the non-adoption of beneficial policies, in policies with unintended consequences or in the loss of policy handles (Alderman et al. 1997).

Family policy for instance may be targeted at different goals. One important objective of most societies certainly is to provide an environment for couples to have children. In order to raise the fertility rate, incentives have to be improved for bearing and rearing children. Another objective is to improve the living conditions of children already born. These two objectives summarize much of conventional family policy measures. Policy measures directly targeted at improving a family's financial situation include child benefits or tax exemptions for raising children. Contrary to the unitary approach to household decision making that assumes income pooling among household members, the bargaining literature tells us that who receives the transfer does indeed matter since the intrafamily utility distribution – not only the distribution between mother and father but also the extent to which children benefit - is affected by the choice of the recipient of the transfer. So policy makers need to know the structure of decision making within the household in order to design appropriate policy measures.

A further objective might be to improve women's status in society in general. While this latter policy goal is usually associated with pursuing equal employment opportunities for both sexes, I argue that promoting equal opportunities of women and men or mothers and fathers in society is a necessary condition for meeting family policy goals. In the preceding chapters it has been shown that raising a family is associated with an unequal time burden for men and women. Still in transition from the breadwinner-cum-homemaker model to the two-earners family, we observe rising female employment, i.e. female participation in a traditionally male time use, at least during the last decades. At the same time we observe only a gradual male involvement in the traditionally female domain of household production. Part of this story is certainly due to different social evaluation of paid and unpaid work and asymmetric bargaining powers associated with both time uses. In Chapter 4 we have learned that, due to the diminishing insurance function of marriage, women enter the labor market at least in part to insure their human capital against the loss of bargaining power and the risk of divorce. But switching from home to market seems like a one-way street. Men only slowly withdraw from the labor market or reduce paid work hours to take over part of the unpaid homework load as we have seen in Chapter 5. This one-way street is strongly supported by institutional settings and social norms. Even if some men inclined to go this way they are rarely encouraged in this by their environment, e.g. male employees being discriminated against for taking parental leave or going on part-time. Hence gender equality in terms of wages and the effective right to a voice in public and private spheres cannot only be regarded as a policy goal by itself but also as a precondition for successful family policy. If society fails to meet the necessary condition for family burdens to be shared equally by men and women, this will have (and already had) severe consequences for women's willingness to have children. Declining birth rates could be interpreted as women being less and less willing to carry the double burden of family work and gainful employment.

Public policy could be usefully aimed at reducing asymmetries in bargaining positions of women and men. Asymmetries are mainly caused by different accumulations of human capital as modeled in the dynamic bargaining model in Chapter 4. The traditional gender-specific specialization within the household implies a growing bargaining power for the spouse specialized in market labor and a diminishing bargaining power for the one specialized in household labor over time. The insurance function of the binding contract marriage imposed by religion, social norms and morals or mutual dependence has been tried to replace with alimony regulations in case of a divorce. These regulations are short-sighted though, since they do not take account of the long-term consequences of the human capital involved. Consequently a possible policy measure would be to grant both spouses joint property rights not only to financial capital but also to *human capital* accumulated during marriage. In case of a divorce the partner with the higher marketable human capital endowment would have to share in the returns to that stock. Such an alimony regulation would help to compensate the asymmetric effects of specialization within the household.

Another starting point would be to prevent the uneven development of relative bargaining positions in the first place. That is to prevent asymmetric loss of human capital associated with raising a family. Effective family policy should provide conditions and incentives that allow both father and mother to combine family work and a job career. Subsidized or free child care services as well as flexible work hours would encourage couples to choose more symmetric time uses.

With regard to the studies on the leisure gap and on the division of housework (Chapters 5 and 6), policy implications can be derived in two directions: Accepting the social structure applied by these models, one conclusion could possibly be to even advocate wage discrimination against women since it seems to be in their interest. After all low-earning women face the smallest leisure pressure. Of course this is only true at the price of a persisting male supremacy and thus does not seem to be an advisable way of tackling the leisure problem. It must also be noted that these results are derived within a static setting. In a dynamic context it will usually be the person with the higher wage rate who is better off in case of a separation, depending on the separation rules. Considering these long-run consequences, employment might also bear human capital effects that have private good character and that are missed in a static model. This dynamic and strategic aspect of female employment has been examined in Chapter 4. It explains why women in spite of low wages might still want to work for pay when considering their expected bargaining position within the household.

Another starting point for policy recommendations would be the abolition of male dominance in society in general, but particularly in the family context. Otherwise the wage gap will never be closed, since it initiates a vicious circle in which women freely choose to work less and accumulate less human capital. This in turns leads to their under-proportionate involvement in public and in economic life and their subordination towards men. The maintenance of a male supremacy together with the structural discrimination of women, e.g. through wage policy, constitute this vicious circle since: "Inasmuch as women's work is consistently linked with lower power, prestige, and material rewards than men's work [...], men continue to enjoy advantages in the control of their time by virtue of their status advantages." (Daly 1996: 153). Hence, the best way to break this vicious circle is to address simultaneously both the wage gap and the dominance question. One example of politically set incentives for a specialization within the household can be found in the present German tax system. Through joint taxation of married couples the second earner's labor force participation is discouraged since his or (in most cases) her earnings are hit by high marginal tax rates (combination of progressive tax rates and "Ehegattensplitting"). The main criticism of this tax policy focuses on its inherent incentive for women to stay out of the labor market. One step towards an equal treatment of men's and women's time use decisions would consequently be a system of individual income taxation.

From longitudinal data we see that there has been a tendency towards equalization of men's and women's contributions to total work. The U.S. leisure gap has been decreasing over the past few decades. From 1975 to 1981 employed women's leisure time increased and their position relative to men improved (Shelton 1992: 116). Robinson and Godbey (1997) also find a rising trend in female private time from 1965 to 1985. Female weekly leisure (including physiological regeneration) rose by 6.8% (7 hours) while male leisure only increased by 3.3% (3 hours). In Sweden women's free time has also been growing due to a decline in women's household work (United Nations 1995).

Policy that would support this trend towards greater equality between women and men includes a shift of the traditional female responsibilities towards both household partners as well as towards society as a whole, i.e. a greater responsibility of those without children to help lower the cost of child-raising to the primary caregivers. For public policy this implies public investments and other measures to supply child care as well as care for the elderly. The leisure gap between women and men can only be diminished when the social roles that are ascribed to gender cease to be associated with different social demands that regulate the distribution of the burden of family work. Facilitating the compatibility of job and raising children together with a promotion of better career opportunities for women would at the same time advance greater gender wage equality. This was shown to be an important determinant of the leisure distribution between fathers and mothers in Chapter 7.

In summary, the empirical analysis of the dissertation strongly supports the position that labor, family or, more specifically, tax policy should not solely rely on the model of the unitary family's time allocation. Moreover, bargaining together with gender issues are an integral part of family decision making and thus need to be incorporated in the analysis of time use within families.

8.3 The next step: cooperative conflicts in a qualitative bargaining framework

The aim of this thesis has been to gain a glimpse into the black box of the family and to analyze the structure of family decision making. In the applications of the bargaining framework used here individuals are assumed to maximize utility under the assumptions of perfect foresight. Family members make decisions on time use and utility distribution given extra-household constraints and social norms that are exogenously determined. Now that we have learned more about the internal organization of the household, further research should be directed towards expanding our focus on the family alone. The spotlight cast on the household should be broadened to include its surrounding institutional setting. Household members should be considered as *interacting* with their extra-household environment. Institutions such as the labor or the goods market, law and the government or the whole system of social values and conventions should no longer be taken as exogenously given but as endogenously determined variables in a changing society.

This is why in recent years formal bargaining models have increasingly been subject to criticism by advocates of a qualitative or institutional bargaining framework (among those Agarwal 1994, 1997, Folbre 1997, Sen 1990a, 1990b)[81]. Those advocates share the principal presumption of the cooperative bargaining model that family members benefit from cooperation by increasing the family pie while the division of this pie will always be subject to conflicts at the same time. But it is argued that formal models neglect the influence of *perceived interests* and *perceived contributions*. Furthermore the

81 For a discussion of the institutional bargaining framework see also Beblo/Soete (2000).

interdependence of social norms and family behavior through the determination of bargaining threat points is pointed out.

The first criticism is addressed to the assumption of individual self-interest and the assumption of clear and unambiguous perceptions of these individual interests. In reality people may not be guided by a clear sense of their own individual welfare, instead they may see their own well-being subsumed in family well-being (Seiz 1995, Sen 1990a, Sen 1990b). The perception of individual contributions to family well-being also plays an important role regarding the division of benefits within the family. If men's productive contributions are perceived greater than women's, for instance because wage income is more visible than home made products, this will certainly influence gender-specific bargaining positions. Furthermore Elizabeth Katz (1997) states that a threat point can only be effective if the "exit option" is a feasible option, that is if the external or internal alternative to cooperation can actually be asserted by the individual. If, due to cultural or religious reasons, divorce is not a feasible option for women, bargaining partners should not be modeled symmetrically. The same applies to spouses' "voices". As Bina Agarwal (1994) pointed out intra-household bargaining might be restricted to limited aspects of family life. Due to social norms women's primary responsibility for household tasks and child care is often excluded from intra-household bargaining. Hence, having a "voice" is a necessary prerequisite for bargaining taking place at all.

Whether bargaining with equal rights can be assumed to take place within the family depends on the prevailing nature of society and its institutions and norms. However, a bargaining setting as it has been used in the models presented can reasonably be assumed for most Western developed countries and thus also for German families who have been the subject of the analyses here. But even if the above criticisms apply, in my opinion this does not imply the complete abandonment of formal bargaining models. One could think of a variation of the cooperative Nash bargaining solution where bargaining weights are adjusted by individual voices and exit options as for instance proposed in Chapter 7. Here the predominant question to be considered is whether bargaining weights or sharing rules are determined by the individuals themselves or whether they are exogeneous to family decision making, certainly a question of culture and gender roles. Alternatively one could think of a non-cooperative setting where partners choose their actions in a prespecified order depending on the consideration of dominance (or exit and voice) as considered in Chapters 5 and 6.

A final point needs to be considered more seriously: "[...] most of what we might wish to understand about power relations must be *assumed* in game-theoretical models; it cannot be *explained* by them." (Seiz 1995: 616). This is where the qualitative bargaining approach proves extremely useful. Agarwal (1997) combines both the institutional and the formal bargaining approach in order to elucidate how power relations are developed and how they are subject to change. She tries to explain how social norms constitute a limit to negotiations and how they form social institutions outside the household. These institutions represented for instance by the labor market, the government or the community have a direct impact on individual bargaining positions within households. Since social norms, values and conventions are culturally determined they can be interpreted as the result of extra-household bargaining of all members of a society. Nancy Folbre (1997) also emphasizes the interdependence of social norms and their effects on institutions and the threat points of intra-household bargaining. Hence, the qualitative bargaining framework considers a whole bargaining circle: Intrahousehold bargaining positions are determined by social institutions that are in turn based on extra-household bargaining in society.

List of figures

List of tables

References

Agarwal, B. (1994): *A Field of One's Own: Gender and Land Rights in South Asia*, Cambridge University Press, Cambridge.

Agarwal, B. (1997): "Bargaining" And Gender Relations: Within And Beyond The Household, *Feminist Economics* 3(1), 1-50.

Alderman, H. et al. (1995): Unitary versus Collective Models of the Household: Is it Time to Shift the Burden of Proof?, *The World Bank Research Observer* 10(1): 1-19.

Alderman, H. and L. Haddad and J. Hoddinott (1997): Policy Issues and Intrahousehold Resource Allocation: Conclusions, in: Haddad, L. and J. Hoddinott and H. Alderman (ed.): *Intrahousehold Resource Allocation in Developing Countries. Models, Methods, and Policy*, Baltimore/London, 275-291.

Althammer, J. and S. Wenzler (1996): Intrafamiliale Zeitallokation, Haushaltsproduktion und Frauenerwerbstätigkeit – Ein mikroökonometrisches Modell zur empirischen Bestimmung des wirtschaftlichen Werts der Hausarbeit, *Jahrbücher für Nationalökonomie und Statistik* 215(4), Stuttgart, 398-418.

Apps, P.F. and R. Rees (1997): Collective Labor Supply and Household Production, *Journal of Political Economy* 105(1): 178-190.

Assenmacher, W. (1990): Das Zeitallokationsproblem des Haushalts, WISU 11, 619-622.

Beblo, M. (1998): *Intrafamily Time Allocation: A Panel-Econometric Analysis of the Division of Housework Time among German Couples*, Discussion Paper 1998/23, Free University of Berlin.

Beblo, M. (1999): *The Leisure Gap between Working Parents. An Empirical Application of an Alternating Offers Game to Intrafamily Time Allocation*, Discussion Paper 1999/19, Free University of Berlin.

Beblo, M. and J.R. Robledo (1999): *Gender, Work and Leisure: A Model of Private Provision of Family Public Goods*, Discussion Paper 1999/32, Free University of Berlin.

Beblo, M. and B. Soete (2000): Der Haushalt als Forschungsgegenstand der ökonomischen Theorie – Macht eine Gender-Analyse Sinn? *Schmollers Jahrbuch* 120(1), 63-92.

Becker, G.S. (1957): *The Economics of Discrimination*, Chicago.

Becker, G.S. (1965): A Theory of the Allocation of Time, *Economic Journal* 75: 493-517.

Becker, G.S. (1973): A Theory of Marriage: Part I, *Journal of Political Economy* 81(4): 813-846.

Becker, G.S. (1974a): A Theory of Marriage: Part II, *Journal of Political Economy* 82(2): S11-S26.

Becker, G.S. (1974b): A Theory of Social Interactions, *Journal of Political Economy* 82(6): 1063-1093.

Becker, G.S. (1976): *The Economic Approach to Human Behavior*, Chicago.

Becker, G.S. (1981a): *A Treatise on the Family*, Chicago.

Becker, G.S. (1981b): Altruism in the Family and Selfishness in the Market Place, *Economica* 48: 1-15.

Becker, G.S. (1982): *Ökonomische Erklärung menschlichen Verhaltens*, Tübingen.

Becker, G.S. (1993): Nobel Lecture: The Economic Way of Looking at Behavior, *Journal of Political Economy* 101(3): 385-409.

Behrman, J.R. (1997): Intrahousehold Distribution and the Family, in: Rosenzweig, M.R. and O. Stark (ed.): *Handbook of Population and Family Economics, Volume 1A*, Amsterdam et al., 125-187.

Ben-Porath, Y. (1980): The F-Connection: Families, Friends, and Firms and the Organization of Exchange, *Population Development Review* 6(1): 1-30.

Bergstrom, T.C. (1996): Economics in a Family Way, *Journal of Economic Literature* 34: 1903-1934.

Bergstrom, T.C. (1997): A Survey of Theories of the Family, in: Rosenzweig, M.R. and O. Stark (ed.): *Handbook of Population and Family Economics, Volume 1A*, Amsterdam et al., 21-79.

Bergstrom, T.C., L. Blume and H. Varian (1986): On the Private Provision of Public Goods, *Journal of Public Economics* 29: 25-49.

Biddle, J.E. and D.S. Hamermesh (1990): Sleep and the Allocation of Time, *Journal of Political Economy* 98(5): 922-943.

Biervert, B. and M. Held (ed.) (1995a): *Zeit in der Ökonomik: Perspektiven für die Theoriebildung*, Frankfurt a. M.

Biervert, B. and M. Held (1995b): Time matters – Zeit in der Ökonomik und Ökonomik der Zeit, in: Biervert, B. and M. Held (ed.): *Zeit in der Ökonomik: Perspektiven für die Theoriebildung*, Frankfurt a. M, 7-32.

Biesecker, A. (1995): Vom (Eigen-)Wert der Zeit – Normative Grundfragen der Zeitökonomik bezüglich einer Neubewertung der Zeit, in: Biervert, B. and M. Held (ed.): *Zeit in der Ökonomik: Perspektiven für die Theoriebildung*, Frankfurt a. M, 190-206.

Binmore, K. (1987): Perfect Equilibria in Bargaining Models, in: Binmore, K. and P. Dasgupta (ed.): *The Economics of Bargaining*, Padstow, 77-105.

Blanke, K. and M. Ehling and N. Schwarz (ed.) (1996): *Zeit im Blickfeld – Ergebnisse einer repräsentativen Zeitbudgeterhebung*, Schriftenreihe des Bundesministeriums für Familie, Senioren, Frauen und Jugend 121, Stuttgart et al.

Blundell, R., F. Laisney and M. Lechner (1993): Alternative Interpretation of Hours Information in an Econometric Model of Labour Supply, *Empirical Economics* 18: 393-415.

Blundell, R. and T. MaCurdy (1998): *Labor Supply: A Review of Alternative Approaches*, Working Paper W98/18, Institute for Fiscal Studies, London.

Blundell, R. et al. (1998): *Collective Labor Supply: Heterogeneity and Nonparticipation*, Working Paper.

Bolin, K. (1996): *An Economic Analysis of Marriage and Divorce*, Lund Economic Studies 62, Lund University.

Bolin, K. (1997): A Family with One Dominating Spouse, in: Persson, I. and Ch. Jonung (ed.): *Economics of the Family and Family Policies*, London, 84-99.

Bourguignon, F. and P.-A. Chiappori (1992): Collective Models of Household Behavior, *European Economic Review* 36: 355-364.

Bourguignon, F. et al. (1993): Intra Household Allocation of Consumption: a Model and some Evidence from French Data, *Annales d'Économie et de Statistique* 29: 137-156.

Brines, J. (1994): Economic Dependency, Gender and the Division of Labor at Home, *American Journal of Sociology* 100: 652-688.

Browning, M. and P.-A. Chiappori (1998): Efficient Intra-Household Allocations: A General Characterization and Empirical Tests, *Econometrica* 66(6): 1241-1278.

Browning, M. and C. Meghir (1991): The Effects of Male and Female Labor Supply on Commodity Demands, *Econometrica* 59(4): 925-951.

Browning, M. et al. (1994): Income and Outcomes: a Structural Model of Intrahousehold Allocation, *Journal of Political Economy* 102(6): 1067-1096.

Buchholz, W., K.A. Konrad and K.E. Lommerud (1997): Stackelberg Leadership and Transfers in Private Provision of Public Goods, *Review of Economic Design* 3: 29-43.

Bürgerliches Gesetzbuch (1957), München/Berlin.

Butrica, B.A. (1998): *The Impact of Future Divorce on Labor Supply and Hours of Women: A Cross-National Comparison of the United States and Germany*, Paper presented at the Third Conference of German Socio-Economic Panel Users, July 1-3 1998,Berlin.

Carlin, P.S. (1991): Intra-Family Bargaining and Time Allocation, *Research in population economics* 7: 215-243.

Chiappori, P.-A. (1988): Rational Household Labor Supply, *Econometrica* 56(1): 63-89.

Chiappori, P.-A. (1992): Collective Labor Supply and Welfare, *Journal of Political Economy* 100(3): 437-467.

Chiappori, P.-A. (1997): Collective Models of Household Behavior: The Sharing Rule Approach, in: Haddad, L. and J. Hoddinott and H. Alderman (ed.): *Intra-household Resource Allocation in Developing Countries. Models, Methods, and Policy*, Baltimore/London, 39-52.

Chiappori, P.-A., B. Fortin and G. Lacroix (1997*): Household Labor Supply, Sharing Rule and the Marriage Market*, Working Paper.

Chiuri, M.C. (1997): *The Unitary vs. the Collective Model of Household Labor Supply with Child Care: An Empirical Test on a Sample of Italian Households*, Discussion Papers in Economics 97(12), University of York.

Daly, K.J. (1996): *Families and Time: Keeping Pace in a Hurried Culture*, Thousand Oaks (California).

Deem, R. (1982): Women, Leisure and Inequality, *Leisure Studies* 1: 29-46.

Del Boca, D. (1997): Intrahousehold Distribution of Resources and Labor Market Participation Decisions, in: Persson, I. and Ch. Jonung (ed.): *Economics of the Family and Family Policies*, London, 65-83.

Diekmann, A. (1994): Hat das steigende Ehescheidungsrisiko das berufliche Engagement von Frauen gefördert?, *Soziale Welt* 45: 83-97.

Diekmann, A. and T. Klein (1991): Bestimmungsgruende des Ehescheidungsrisikos. Eine empirische Untersuchung mit den Daten des sozio-oekonomischen Panels, *Koelner Zeitschrift fuer Soziologie und Sozialpsychologie* 43: 271-290.

Diekmann, A. and P. Mitter (1984): *Methoden zur Analyse von Zeitverläufen*, Stuttgart.

Dobbelsteen, S. and P. Kooreman (1997): Financial Management, Bargaining and Efficiency within the Household; an Empirical Analysis, *De Economist* 145(3): 345-366.

Doss, C. (1996): Testing among Models of Intrahousehold Resource Allocation, *World development* 24(10): 1597-1609.

Ehling, M. (1996): Arbeitsfreie Zeit – Freizeit heute, in: Blanke, K. and M. Ehling and N. Schwarz (ed.): *Zeit im Blickfeld – Ergebnisse einer repräsentativen Zeitbudgeter-hebung*. Schriftenreihe des Bundesministeriums für Familie, Senioren, Frauen und Jugend 121, Stuttgart et al., 219-236.

Firestone, J. and B.A. Shelton (1994): A Comparison of Women's and Men's Leisure Time: Subtle Effects of the Double Day, *Leisure Sciences* 16: 45-60.

Fleck, S.E. (1996): *Non-Cooperative Bargaining and Power in the Household. Evidence from Honduras*, Paper presented at the 1996 Conference on Feminist Economics, June 21-23, American University, Washington, DC.

Folbre, N. (1984): Market Opportunities, Genetic Endowments, and Intrafamily Resource Distribution: Comment, *American Economic Review* 74(3): 518-520.

Folbre, N. (1994): *Who Pays for the Kids? Gender and the Structure of Constraints*, London.

Folbre, N. (1997): Gender Coalitions: Extrafamily Influences on Intrafamily Inequalities, in: Haddad, L. and J. Hoddinott and H. Alderman (ed.): *Intrahousehold Resource Allocation in Developing Countries. Models, Methods, and Policy*, Baltimore/London, 263-274.

Fortin, B. and G. Lacroix (1997): A Test of the Unitary and Collective Models of Household Labor Supply, *Economic Journal* 107: 933-955.

Franz, W. (1996): *Arbeitsmarktoekonomik*, Berlin/Heidelberg.

Gaugler, E., E. Schach and M. Vollmer (1984): *Wiedereingliederung von Frauen in qualifizierte Berufstätigkeit nach längerer Berufsunterbrechung*, Mannheim.

Graham, J.W. and C.A. Green (1984): Estimating the Parameters of a Household Production Function with Joint Products, *Review of Economics and Statistics* 66: 277-282.

Grammig, J. (1996): *Nachfrage-Restriktionen des individuellen Arbeitsangebot: Eine mikroökonometrische Analyse für die USA und Deutschland*, Frankfurt a. M./New York.

Gray, J.S. (1998): Divorce-Law Changes, Household Bargaining, and Married Women's Labor Supply, *American Economic Review* 88(3): 628-642.

Greene, W.H. (1993): *Econometric Analysis*, New York.

Gronau, R. (1973): The Intrafamily Allocation of Time: The Value of the Housewives' Time, *American Economic Review* 63: 634-651.

Gronau, R. (1977): Leisure, Home Production, and Work: The Theory of the Allocation of Time Revisited, *Journal of Political Economy* 85(6): 1099-1123.

Grossman, S. and O. Hart (1986): The Costs and Benefits of Ownership: A theory of Vertical and Lateral Integration, *Journal of Political Economy* 94: 691-719.

Hadfield, G.K. (1999): A Coordination Model of the Sexual Division of Labor, *Journal of Economic Behavior and Organization* 40: 125-153.

Harsanyi, J.C. (1977): *Rational Behaviour and Bargaining Equilibrium in Games and Social Situations*, Cambridge.

Hart, O. and J. Moore (1990): Property Rights and the Nature of the Firm, *Journal of Political Economy* 98: 1119-1158.

Haurin, D.R. (1989): Women's Labor Market Reactions to Family Disruptions, *Review of Economics and Statistics*: 54-61.

Hausman, J.A. and W.E. Taylor (1981): Panel Data and Unobservable Individual Effects, *Econometrica* 49: 1377-1398.

Heckman, J. (1979): Sample Selection Bias as a Specification Error, *Econometrica* 47(1), 153-162.

Heckman, J. (1980): Sample Selection Bias as a Specification Error with an Application to the Estimation of Labor Supply, in: Smith, J.P. (ed.): *Female Labor Supply: Theory and Estimation*, Princeton, 206-248.

Hersch, J. and L.S. Stratton (1994): Housework, Wages, and the Division of Housework Time for Employed Spouses, *American Economic Review (Papers and Proceedings)* 84(2): 120-125.

Hirshleifer, J. (1977): Shakespeare vs. Becker on Altruism: The Importance of Having the Last Word, *Journal of Economic Literature* 15: 500-502.

Hochschild, A. (1989): *The Second Shift*, New York.

Hoddinott, J., H. Alderman and L. Haddad (1997): Testing Competing Models of Intrahousehold Allocation, in: Hoddinott, J., H. Alderman and L. Haddad (ed.): *Intrahousehold Resource Allocation in Developing Countries. Models, Methods, and Policy*, Baltimore/London, 129-141.

Holz, E. (1998): *Zeitverwendung in Deutschland*, Schriftenreihe" Spektrum Bundesstatistik ", Statistisches Bundesamt (ed.), Wiesbaden, manuscript (forthcoming 1999).

Horney, M.J. and M.B. McElroy (1988): The Household Allocation Problem: Empirical Results from a Bargaining Model, *Research in Population Economics* 6: 15-38.

Hsiao, C. (1989): *Analysis of Panel Data*, Cambridge.

Huber, J. and G. Spitze (1983): *Sex Stratification: Children, Housework and Jobs*, New York.

Johnson, W.R. and J. Skinner (1986): Labor Supply and Marital Separation, *American Economic Review* 76(3): 455-469.

Jones, C.W. (1983): The Mobilization of Women's Labor for Cash Crop Production: A Game Theoretic Approach, *American Journal of Agricultural Economics* 65(5): 1049-1054.

Judge, G.G. et al. (1988): *Introduction to the Theory and Practice of Econometrics*, New York.

Juster, F.T. (1985a): A Note on Changes in Time Use, in: Juster, F.T. and F.P. Stafford (ed.): *Time, Goods and Well-Being*, Ann Arbor, 313-332.

Juster, F.T. (1985b): Investments of Time by Men and Women, in: Juster, F.T. and F.P. Stafford (ed.): *Time, Goods and Well-Being*, Ann Arbor, 177-204.

Katz, E. (1997): The Intra-Household Economics of Voice and Exit, *Feminist Economics* 3(3): 25-46.

Killingsworth, M.R. (1983): *Labor Supply*, New York.

Killingsworth, M.R. and J.J. Heckman (1986): Female Labor Supply: A Survey, in: Ashenfelter, O. and R. Layard (ed.): *Handbook of Labor Economics 1*, New York, 103-204.

Konrad, K.A. and K.E. Lommerud (1995): Family Policy with Non-Cooperative Families, *Scandinavian Journal of Economics* 97: 581-601.

Konrad, K.A. and K.E. Lommerud (1996): *The Bargaining Family Revisited*, CEPR Discussion Paper 1312.

Layard, R., M. Barton and A. Zabalza (1980): Married Women's Participation and Hours, *Economica* 47(185): 51-72.

Lehrer, E. and M. Nerlove (1981): The Labor Supply and Fertility Behavior of Married Women: A Three-Period Model, *Research in Population Economics* 3: 123-145.

Leuthold, J. (1968): An Empirical Study of Formula Income Transfers and the Work Decisions of the Poor, *Journal of Human Resources* 3: 312-323.

Lommerud, K.E. (1989): Marital Division of Labor with Risk of Divorce: The Role of "Voice" Enforcement of Contracts, *Journal of Labor Economics* 7(1): 113-127.

Lommerud, K.E. (1997): Battles of the Sexes: Non-Cooperative Games in the Theory of the Family, in: Persson, I. and Ch. Jonung (ed.): *Economics of the Family and Family Policies*, London, 44-62.

Lundberg, S. (1988): Labor Supply of Husbands and Wives: A Simultaneous Equations Approach, *Review of Economics and Statistics*: 224-235.

Lundberg, S. and R.A. Pollak (1993): Separate Spheres Bargaining and the Marriage Market, *Journal of Political Economy* 101(6): 988-1010.

Lundberg, S. and R.A. Pollak (1994): Non-Cooperative Bargaining Models of Marriage, *American Economic Review (Papers and Proceedings)* 84(2): 132-137.

Lundberg, S. and R.A. Pollak (1996): Bargaining and Distribution in Marriage, *Journal of Economic Perspectives* 10(4): 139-158.

Lundberg, S., R.A. Pollak. and T.J. Wales (1997): Do Husbands and Wives Pool their Resources? Evidence from the United Kingdom Child Benefit, *Journal of Human Resources* 32(3): 463-480.

Manser, M. and M. Brown (1979): Bargaining Analysis of Household Decisions, in: Lloyd, C.B. and E.S. Andrews and C.L. Golroy (ed.): *Women in the labor market*, New York.

Manser, M. and M. Brown (1980): Marriage and Household Decision Making: A Bargaining Analysis, *International Economic Review* 21(1): 31-44.

McElroy, M.B. (1990): The Empirical Content of Nash-Bargained Household Behavior, *Journal of Human Resources* 25(4): 559-583.

McElroy, M.B. and M.J. Horney (1981): Nash-Bargained Household Decisions: Toward a Generalization of the Theory of Demand, *International Economic Review* 22(2): 333-349.

Marx, K. (1857/58): *Grundrisse der Kritik der Politischen Ökonomie (Rohentwurf)*, Berlin 1953, 89.

Marx, K. (1857/58, translation from 1973): *Grundrisse: Foundations of the Critique of Political Economy (Rough Draft)*, Middlesex, 173.

Mincer, J. (1962): Labor Force Participation of Married Women, in: *Aspects of Labor Economics*, National Bureau of Economic Research, Princeton, 63-105.

Mroz, T.A. (1987): The Sensitivity of an Empirical Model of Married Women's Hours of Work to Economic and Statistical Assumptions, *Econometrica* 55(4): 765-799.

Nash, J. (1953): Two-Person Bargaining Games, *Econometrica* 21: 128-140.

Ott, N. (1992): *Intrafamily Bargaining and Household Decisions*, Berlin/Heidelberg.

Ott, N. (1993): Die Rationalität innerfamilialer Entscheidungen als Beitrag zur Diskri-minierung weiblicher Arbeit, in: Grözinger, G. and R. Schubert and J. Backhaus (ed.): *Jenseits von Diskriminierung. Zu den institutionellen Bedingungen weiblicher Arbeit in Beruf und Familie*, Marburg, 113-146.

Ott, N. (1995): Fertility and Division of Work in the Family: A Game Theoretic Model of Household Decisions, in: Kuiper, E. and J. Sap (ed.): *Out of the Margin*, London/New York, 80-99.

Ott, N. (1998): Der familienökonomische Ansatz von Gary S. Becker, in: Pies, I. and M. Leschke (ed.): *Gary Beckers ökonomischer Imperialismus*, Tübingen, 63-90.

Ott, N. (1999): Eigenproduktion versus Dienstleistungen im Haushalt. Zum ökonomischen Wert der Hausarbeit, in: Beblo, M. and G. Krell and K. Schneider and B. Soete (ed.): *Ökonomie und Geschlecht: Volks- und betriebswirtschaftliche Analysen mit der Kategorie Geschlecht*, München/Mering, 35-52.

Parkman, A.M. (1992): Unilateral Divorce and the Labor-Force Participation Rate of Married Women, Revisited, *American Economic Review*: 671-678.

Peters, H.E. (1986): Marriage and Divorce: Informational Constraints and Private Contracting, *American Economic Review*, 437-454.

Phipps, S. and P.S. Burton (1995): Social/Institutional Variables and Behavior within Households: An Empirical Test using the Luxembourg Income Study, *Feminist Economics* 1(1): 151-174.

Pollak, R.A. (1985): A Transaction Cost Approach to Families and Households, *Journal of Economic Literature* 23: 581-608.

Pollak, R.A. (1994): For Better or Worse: The Roles of Power in Models of Distribution within Marriage, *American Economic Review (Papers and Proceedings)* 84(2): 148-152.

Projektgruppe Sozio-oekonomisches Panel (1995): Das Sozio-oekonomische Panel (SOEP) im Jahre 1994, *Vierteljahreshefte zur Wirtschaftsforschung* 64(1): 5-13.

Puhani, P.A. (1997): *Foul or Fair? The Heckman Correction for Sample Selection and Its Critique. A Short Survey*, ZEW-Discussion Paper 97-07E, Mannheim.

Radke, P. (1996): *Zeitallokation im Familienzusammenhang: Modellierung des Arbeitsangebots unter Einbezug des sozialen Tausches*, Frankfurt a. M.

Rendtel, U. (1992): *On the Choice of a Selection-Model when Estimating Regression Models with Selectivity*, DIW-Discussion Paper 53, Berlin.

Robinson, J. and G. Godbey (1997): *Time for Life. The Surprising Ways Americans Use Their Time*, Pennsylvania.

Rosenzweig, M. and T.P. Schultz (1982): Market Opportunities, Genetic Endowments, and Intrafamily Resource Distribution: Child Survival in Rural India, *American Economic Review* 72(4): 803-815.

Rosenzweig, M. and T.P. Schultz (1984): Market Opportunities, Genetic Endowments, and Intrafamily Resource Distribution: Reply, *American Economic Review* 74(4): 521-522.

Rubinstein, A. (1982): Perfect Equilibrium in a Bargaining Model, *Econometrica* 50: 97-109.

Samuelson, P.A. (1956): Social Indifference Curves, *Quarterly Journal of Economics* 70(1): 1-22.

Schäfer, D. and N. Schwarz (1996). Der Wert der unbezahlten Arbeit der privaten Haushalte – Das Satellitensystem Haushaltsproduktion, in: Blanke, K. and M. Ehling and N. Schwarz (ed.): *Zeit im Blickfeld – Ergebnisse einer repräsentativen Zeitbudgeterhebung.* Schriftenreihe des Bundesministeriums für Familie, Senioren, Frauen und Jugend 121, Stuttgart et al., 15-69.

Schultz, T.P. (1990): Testing the Neoclassical Model of Family Labor Supply and Fertility, *Journal of Human Resources* 25(4): 635-664.

Seiz, J.A. (1995): Bargaining Models, Feminism, and Institutionalism, *Journal of Economic Issues* 21(2): 609-619.

Sen, A. (1990a): Cooperation, Inequality, and the Family, in: Folbre, N. (ed.): *The Economics of the Family*, Cheltenham/Brookfield, 171-186.

Sen, A. (1990b): Gender and Cooperative Conflicts, in: Tinker, I. (ed.): *Persistent Inequalities - Women and Development*, Oxford/ New York/ Toronto, 195-223.

Senauer, B. (1990): The Impact of the Value of Women's Time on Food and Nutrition, in: Tinker, I. (ed.): *Persistent Inequalitys - Women and World Development*, Oxford/ New York/ Toronto, 150-161.

Shaked, A. and J. Sutton (1984): Involuntary Unemployment as a Perfect Equilibrium in a Bargaining Model, *Econometrica* 52(6): 1351-1364.

Shaw, S. (1992): Dereifying Family Leisure: An Examination of Women's and Men's Everyday Experiences and Perceptions of Family Time, *Leisure Sciences* 14: 271-286.

Shelton, B.A. (1992): *Women, Men and Time. Gender Differences in Paid Work, Housework and Leisure.* Contributions in Women's Studies 127, Westport CT.

Statistisches Bundesamt (ed.) (1990): *Familien heute. Strukturen, Verläufe und Einstellungen.* Stuttgart.

Statistisches Bundesamt (ed.) (1995): *Die Zeitverwendung der Bevölkerung: Ergebnisse der Zeitbudgeterhebung 1991/92*, Tabellenbände I-IV, Wiesbaden.

Statistisches Bundesamt (ed.) (1997): *Statistisches Jahrbuch 1997*, Wiesbaden.

Statistisches Bundesamt (ed.) (1998a): *Im Blickpunkt: Frauen in Deutschland*, Wiesbaden.

Statistisches Bundesamt (ed.) (1998b): *Löhne und Gehälter*, Fachserie 16, Wiesbaden.

Strauss, J. and D. Thomas (1996): Human Resources - Empirical Modeling of Household and Family Decisions, in: Behrman, J. and T.N. Srinivasan (eds.): *Handbook of Development Economics, Volume IIIA*, Amsterdam, 1883-2023.

Strober, M.H. and C.B. Weinberg (1980): Strategies by Working and Nonworking Wives to Reduce Time Pressures, *Journal of Consumer Research* 6: 338-348.

Thomas, D. (1990): Intra-Household Resource Allocation: an Inferential Approach, *Journal of Human Resources* 25(4): 635-664.

Thomas, D. (1993): The Distribution of Income and Expenditure within the Household, *Annales d'Économie et de Statistique* 29: 109-136.

Thomas, D. (1994): Like Father Like Son, Like Mother Like Daughter: Parental Resources and Child Height, *Journal of Human Resources* 29(4): 950-989.

Thomas, D. (1997): Incomes, Expenditures, and Health Outcomes: Evidence on Intrahousehold Resource Allocation, in: Haddad, L. and J. Hoddinott and H. Alderman (ed.): *Intrahousehold Resource Allocation in Developing Countries. Models, Methods, and Policy*, Baltimore/London, 142-164.

Thomas, D. and C.-L. Chen (1994): *Income Shares and Shares of Income: Empirical Tests of Models of Household Resource Allocations*, Santa Monica (California): RAND, mimeo.

Tiefenthaler, J. (1999): The Sectoral Labor Supply of Married Couples in Brazil: Testing the Unitary Model of Household Behavior, *Journal of Population Economics* 12 (4): 591-606.

Udry, C. (1996): Gender, Agricultural Production, and the Theory of the Household, *Journal of Political Economy* 104(5): 1010-1046.

United Nations (1995): *Human Development Report 1995*, United Nations Development Programme, Oxford, 87-98.

Wagner, G. and R.V. Burkhauser and F. Behringer (1993): The English Language Public Use File of the German Socio-Economic Panel Study, *Journal of Human Resources* 28(2): 429-433.

Walker, I and Y. Zhu (1999): *The Labour Supply of Married Couples and the Effects of Intra-Household Redistribution*, Keele University, mimeo.

Wells, R. and M. Maher (1996): *Time and Surplus Allocation Within Marriage*, Research Paper Series 1372, Stanford University.

Woolley, F.R. (1988): *A Non-Cooperative Model of Family Decision Making*, Working Paper TIDI 125, London.

Woolley, F.R. (1993): The Feminist Challenge to Neoclassical Economics, *Cambridge Journal of Economics* 17(4): 485-500.

Woolley, F.R. (1996): *Tax-Benefit Policy and the Intra-Household Allocation of Resources*, Paper presented at: The Family: Legal, Economic and Policy Perspectives, June 7-8, 1996, Vancouver.

Zimmermann, K.F. (1985): *Familienökonomie - Theoretische und empirische Untersuchungen zur Frauenerwerbstätigkeit und Geburtenentwicklung*, Berlin/Heidelberg.

Contributions to Economics

Katharina Müller/Andreas Ryll/
Hans-Jürgen Wagener (Eds.)
Transformation of Social Security: Pensions in Central-Eastern Europe
1999. ISBN 3-7908-1210-2

Stefan Traub
Framing Effects in Taxation
1999. ISBN 3-7908-1240-4

Pablo Coto-Millán
Utility and Production
1999. ISBN 3-7908-1153-X

Frank Riedel
Imperfect Information and Investor Heterogeneity in the Bond Market
2000. ISBN 3-7908-1247-1

Kirsten Ralf
Business Cycles
2000. ISBN 3-7908-1245-5

Michele Bagella/
Leonardo Becchetti (Eds.)
The Competitive Advantage of Industrial Districts
2000. ISBN 3-7908-1254-4

Frank Bohn
Monetary Union and Fiscal Stability
2000. ISBN 3-7908-1266-8

Jaime Behar
Cooperation and Competition in a Common Market
2000. ISBN 3-7908-1280-3

Michael Malakellis
Integrated Macro-Micro-Modelling Under Rational Expectations
2000. ISBN 3-7908-1274-9

Stefan Baumgärtner
Ambivalent Joint Production and the Natural Environment
2000. ISBN 3-7908-1290-0

Henri Capron, Wim Meeusen
(Eds.)
The National Innovation System of Belgium
2000. ISBN 3-7908-1308-7

Tobias Miarka
Financial Intermediation and Deregulation
2000. ISBN 3-7908-1307-9

Chisato Yoshida
Illegal Immigration and Economic Welfare
2000. ISBN 3-7908-1315-X

Nikolaus Thumm
Intellectual Property Rights
2000. ISBN 3-7908-1329-X

Max Keilbach
Spatial Knowledge Spillovers and the Dynamics of Agglomeration and Regional Growth
2000. ISBN 3-7908-1321-4

Alexander Karmann (Ed.)
Financial Structure and Stability
2000. ISBN 3-7908-1332-X

Joos P. A. van Vugt/Jan M. Peet
(Eds.)
Social Security and Solidarity in the European Union
2000. ISBN 3-7908-1334-6

Johannes Bröcker/Hayo Herrmann
(Eds.)
Spatial Change and Interregional Flows in the Integrating Europe
2001. ISBN 3-7908-1344-3

Kirstin Hubrich
Cointegration Analysis in a German Monetary System
2001. ISBN 3-7908-1352-4

Nico Heerink et al. (Eds.)
Economic Policy and Sustainable Land Use
2001. ISBN 3-7908-1351-6

Friedel Bolle/Michael Carlberg
(Eds.)
Advances in Behavioral Economics
2001. ISBN 3-7908-1358-3

Volker Grossmann
Inequality, Economic Growth, and Technological Change
2001. ISBN 3-7908-1364-8

Thomas Riechmann
Learning in Economics
2001. ISBN 3-7908-1384-2